REWILDING
EARTH
UNPLUGGED

REWILDING EARTH UNPLUGGED

Best of Rewilding Earth 2018

Edited by John Davis & Susan Morgan

To Sandy
For more wild adventures,
Susan
John

Rewilding Institute

Essex Editions
Post Office Box 25
Essex, New York 12936
essexeditions.com
contact@essexeditions.com

Table Of Contents

INTRODUCTION: REWILDING DISTILLED

Rewilding, in essence, is giving the land back to wildlife and wildlife back to the land. It is restoring natural processes and species, then stepping back so the land can express its own will. Rewilding often focuses on the apex predators—like wolves, great cats, crocodiles, sharks, and salmon—and other keystone species that tend to need wild space and be lost quickly in domesticated or exploited lands and waters. Rewilding thus aims for restoration at a grand scale, the scale of conservation needed by wide-ranging species. *Rewilding Earth* celebrates, though, restoration efforts at all scales and in all places, while always aiming for as big and wild and connected and biologically complete as possible.

The term 'rewilding' was coined by Dave Foreman, co-founder of *Wild Earth* magazine and The Wildlands Project, in the early 1990s. The concept of rewilding was further articulated by Michael Soulé and Reed Noss in their classic *Wild Earth* paper "Rewildling and Biodiversity: Complementary Goals for Continental Conservation" in 1998. Other leading conservation biologists, including John Terborgh, Jim Estes, Susan Morse, John Laundre, and Cristina Eisenberg, have further elucidated the rewilding concept and added to its scientific rigor through their books (some of them available through our Rewilding Bookstore), articles, and classes.

As these and other naturalists and conservation biologists have shown, top carnivores are not just pretty faces or effective icons for endangered species campaigns; they are central players in healthy ecosystems. Removal of apex predators has had cascading effects ('trophic cascades' is a term some biologists use) in terrestrial and aquatic ecosystems around the world. To give just two from a growing litany of examples: Since the eradication of pumas and gray and red wolves from the eastern United States, white-tail deer have become unnaturally abundant and sedentary, and they are now browsing eastern deciduous forests to the ground. In the western US, since the extirpation of wolves, elk and/or mule deer are similarly overpopulating and over-browsing aspen groves and other sensitive plant communities. The science clearly shows that restoring the missing predators is essential to restoring the plant communities.

Rewilding, though, is as poetic an idea as it is scientific, and may sometimes be best expounded through art and direct experience on the ground. A painting of a gray wolf pack taking an old lame moose, or better yet the thrill of watching that scene through binoculars in real life, may realize the rewilding concept better than any scientific paper could.

Thanks to the good work of conservationists and restorationists the world over, rewilding is happening in many places. Rewilding Europe has helped restore beavers to parts of Scotland, wolves to many parts of mainland Europe, and lynx to Iberia. River liberators have removed dams and reopened salmon runs from the Kennebec and Penobscot Rivers in Maine, the Elwha River in Washington, the Eklutna River in Alaska, and hundreds of other places. Wolves have been famously restored to the Greater Yellowstone Ecosystem and from there have recolonized as far away as northern California—to the redounding benefit of riparian forests and the many creatures who depend upon those lush ecosystems. Peregrine falcons and bald eagles are now numerous again in much of North America, since successful restoration programs and the banning of DDT many years ago; even the highly imperiled California condor is now soaring again over some of its old southwestern strongholds. Cheetah and lion restoration efforts have succeeded in some parts of southern Africa. Conservation Land Trust is systematically restoring extirpated species to Argentina's vast Iberá wetlands, with

Jaguars, largest of the Western Hemisphere's many cat species, once ranged across much of the US Southwest, as well as Mexico and Central and South America. Their attempts to recolonize habitats north of Mexico are now imperiled by the US border wall and proposed mines in southern Arizona. © Robin Silver Photography

pampas deer and lowland tapir and giant anteater already back out there and jaguars being raised for release. Tallgrass prairie and savanna naturalists have restored many sites in the Midwest US. Wildlands philanthropists with the Southern Plains Land Trust and the American Prairie Reserve in southeast Colorado and eastern Montana are piecing together big wild cores and repopulating them with prairie dogs, bison, and other extirpated species.

One of the great, if accidental, experiments in rewilding is New York's Adirondack Park. Here, just hours north of Wall Street, in a landscape largely denuded a century ago by timber and railroad companies, state land protection has allowed the return of beaver, fisher, river otter, moose and other once-extirpated species to forests approaching old-growth stature again. Now the land anxiously awaits the return of puma and gray wolf, to ensure its recovering forests remain healthy and diverse; and may also benefit from the planting in old fields of disease-resistant American Chestnut and native oaks and hickories, helping keep the forest resilient in the face of human-forced climate warming.

Carolyn Frazier's important book *Rewilding the World* gives many more examples, as does *Rewilding Earth* (rewilding. org), The Rewilding Institute's online pub, and this our first annual print anthology, *Rewilding Earth Unplugged*. The book that best summarizes priorities for continental conservation and restoration is Dave Foreman's *Rewilding North America*.

This little anthology, *Rewilding Earth Unplugged,* proved tougher than we expected to produce, not for lack of material but quite the opposite. In our first full year of publication, *Rewilding Earth* ran nearly a hundred articles and several times that many pieces of art. Choosing from these for our best-of annual print book was agonizing. In the end, we decided to run original pieces, not reprints, and to choose a broad cross-section of the many inspiring articles we received. We urge all readers to go to rewilding.org to find additional articles (easy to locate with our website's search function and the index provided at end of this book), as well as to share their—*your*—own rewilding success stories and lessons with us. We also call your attention to our *Rewilding Earth* podcast series, which has already given voice to a score of wilderness and wildlife luminaries, and aims to put out a podcast interview each week. If you are involved in a rewilding project, please send us a short description and contact information on the lead players for inclusion in our future Rewilding Directory.

We dutifully note here that views expressed are the authors' own, not necessarily shared by other authors and groups in this anthology or in our online pub. Of course, *Rewilding Earth* editors try to ensure that every contribution furthers the cause of protecting and restoring wild places and creatures, but within this broad movement are many strains of thought and even divergent opinions. How to compassionately and effectively address the human overpopulation crisis and just what constitutes 'rewilding' are two broad questions that generate lively debates, which we are happy to share (provided they are respectful and helpful) in our pages.

If sharp-eyed, editorially-minded readers see inconsistencies in style here (as, for instance, with capitalization of species names or public lands designations), please think us not careless but understand that we *RE* editors ask for consistency within articles but let authors choose their own styles. If you wonder about the ecological effects of printing this book, please know we sought to minimize the number of trees cut to produce it by printing a minimum number and being in a print-on-demand basis, which makes difficult the use of recycled paper. Rather than printing a large number on recycled paper, we are printing only the number we can readily distribute. There are many paradoxes in modern publishing, and the difficulty of going recycled if you go small is one. Please make sure your copy of *Rewilding Earth Unplugged* gets read by multiple people, so the small number of trees sacrificed will have died for a good cause.

Grateful thanks are due to all the authors and artists, activists and scientists, and financial and temporal donors, who have given generously to The Rewilding Institute and enabled us to start *Rewilding Earth* on a path similar to the late great journal *Wild Earth*. Extra special thanks are due to our senior editor Susan Morgan and Essex Editions editors Katie Shepard and George Davis, who provided much of the inspired creativity and hard labor to pull this anthology together. Equal gratitude goes to our business sponsors: Biohabitats, Essex Editions, Foundation Earth, Kahtoola, and Patagonia. Please see their sponsorship pages in this book, and if you have an ecologically-friendly business, please consider placing an ad in or otherwise sponsoring *Rewilding Earth*.

Let's learn from the many scientists and visionaries in *Rewilding Earth* and start giving back to the land. The forests are hungry for wolves and pumas; the grasslands hungry for bison and wolves; the rivers hungry for salmon and eel; the seas hungry for whales and sharks. The answer to the overarching crisis of our time—extinction—is rewilding, at all scales, from your back forty to Patagonia's vast steppe.

—John Davis, *Rewilding Earth* editor,
writing from Split Rock Wildway,
Adirondack Park

WILDLANDS
PHILANTHROPY

Blue Mountain Lake is central, geographically and scenically, to New York's great Adirondack Park. © Kevin Raines

BRINGING BACK THE AMERICAN SERENGETI

BY NICOLE ROSMARINO, SOUTHERN PLAINS
LAND TRUST

Immerse yourself in the natural history of North America's grasslands, and you'll daydream about going back in time to see the massive herds of bison and pronghorn that made the Great Plains an exciting ecotourism destination for British aristocrats in the 1800s, massive prairie dog colonies stretching over thousands of square miles, and lesser prairie-chickens conducting their ancient and provocative mating dances. In that daydream, you'll not only ache to view these spectacular wildlife phenomena but to make sure they persist for millennia to come.

It turns out you don't need time travel. Sure, reach back to that rich history for inspiration and to guard against a shifting baseline, where we settle for less than what used to be. But, in the southern Great Plains right now, we can protect an amazing array of uniquely North American wildlife through the establishment of private wildlife refuges. Just buy the land under the critters' feet. Use the free market and private property rights to advance permanent, tangible conservation. The opportunity is immense, given that the region has seen declining human populations since the Dust Bowl of the 1930s, much of the habitat remains intact, and land prices are low.

Denizens of North America's grassland prairie, bison thrive in SPLT's network of shortgrass prairie preserves. © Sean Boggs for Environmental Defense Fund

The shortgrass prairies of the southern Great Plains provide, in some senses, a step back in time. The sheer extent of sweeping, intact grasslands embodies outstanding scenic and conservation values. The gently rolling landscape challenges the notion of a flat and empty land: its relief can hide a herd of pronghorn or an oasis of grandmother cottonwood trees. Where the swells lessen, you might encounter a lively, bustling prairie dog town. Prairie dogs are the MVPs of the shortgrass prairie, creating habitat for hundreds of wildlife species. Just follow the hawks and badgers: they'll show you the prairie dog colony hotspots.

I think of the prairie as a place that breaks your heart one moment and makes it sing the next. There's a melancholy here, and I think it's because we all know, deep down, how much we've lost. Yet, the celebration is in what remains and the promise of returning the whole. Much of the region has never been plowed, and most of the animal species assemblage persists or might feasibly be reintroduced. The coyote provides a defiant reminder of the enduring wild spirit of this place.

While reference to the Great Plains as America's Serengeti is an imperfect analogy, it is intended as a way to communicate that our region is important and worth preserving—on the order of the African Serengeti. Dan Flores alerts us to that in his award-winning book, *American Serengeti: The Last Big Animals of the Great Plains,* where he chronicles the dazzling animal abundance that rendered John James Audubon speechless in the 1840s. The tale that then unfolded was a sorrowful one: where species after delightful species was hunted to the very brink of extinction and sometimes beyond. They string together, bison-pronghorn-elk-grizzly bear-grey wolf, with the drivers of disappearance being market pressures and a quest to tame the wilderness.

But there's a spark of hope today: bison can be reintroduced, pronghorn have held on, and elk can find the way back to their prairie home from the mountains. Prairie dogs can flourish if we just spare them from poisons and guns. The large predators are more of a challenge, given the intolerance they face even now in forest and mountain landscapes outside of our region, including those with large swaths of federal lands.

Private Land Refuges In The Southern Plains

We cannot depend on public lands in the southern Great Plains to preserve biodiversity, as they are broadly utilized for livestock grazing and energy development. 90% of the land within our region is private, and the wildlife is often heavily hunted on public and private lands alike. Large-scale private refuges are vital to prevent the conversion of native grasslands to crop agriculture, energy development, and other land uses that would irreversibly alter shortgrass prairie plant communities. **Equally important is preservation of wildlife: we can't just protect the habitat— we need to protect the wild animals and plants that bring the landscape to life.**

The need for large protected areas is increasingly recognized by scientists across the world, especially the Pulitzer Prize-winning author and scientist Edward O. Wilson. In *Half-Earth: Our Planet's Fight for Life,* Dr. Wilson advocates that 50% of the planet be protected in preserves to prevent biodiversity loss. Less than 1% of the Great Plains is conserved. We'd better get busy.

The Southern Plains Land Trust (SPLT) is creating and protecting a network of shortgrass prairie preserves, to ensure the future of all native animals and plants in the southern Great Plains (a similar effort is underway in the northern Great Plains by the American Prairie Reserve.) Thus far, SPLT's preserve

11

network contains more than 25,000 acres. Unlike many other land trusts, we prefer to purchase and hold land ourselves so that we can manage it for biodiversity. We own 23,000 acres and hold conservation easements on an additional 2,000 acres.

Our largest property is Heartland Ranch Nature Preserve in southeastern Colorado. At more than 18,000 acres, Heartland Ranch is nearly 30 square miles in size and larger than the city of Boulder, Colorado, and any one of Colorado's state parks. SPLT has reintroduced bison to Heartland Ranch, thus putting back in place the US National Mammal. This keystone species maintains grasslands by ripping out shrubs, creating a mosaic of taller and shorter grass areas that benefit a suite of prairie birds, and its wallowing provides microhabitats for prairie wildflowers and ephemeral pools for spadefoot toads.

Historically, bison and black-tailed prairie dogs were bookends of biodiversity on the shortgrass prairie. Heartland contains at least ten prairie dog colonies, which we are protecting from threats so that one day we can reintroduce the black-footed ferret, one of North America's most endangered mammals. In the meantime, black-tailed prairie dogs themselves urgently need safe refuge, given their decline by about 95% from historic population levels. They have long been persecuted by agricultural operators, often in tandem with government agencies, given the perception that prairie dogs compete with cattle for forage. While prairie dogs no doubt consume plants, more than four decades of science now shows that under some circumstances they can benefit livestock by reducing shrubs, enhancing nutritional value and succulence of forage, and increasing the ability of soils and plants to absorb precipitation. Yet, the persecution of prairie dogs continues.

This is bad news not only for prairie dogs but also for the wildlife that depends on them. Like the bison, prairie dogs are a keystone species. Alongside the black-footed ferret, imperiled wildlife that benefit from prairie dogs and the habitat they create include the swift fox, burrowing owl, mountain plover, and ferruginous hawk. These associated species have all been adversely affected by the dramatic decline in prairie dog populations. Absolute refuge is a must for the present and future of the prairie dog ecosystem.

By refuge, we mean no hunting or exploitation of native wildlife. At SPLT, we think that's the least we can offer the region's wildlife, many of whose populations are a shadow of their former selves. Think of pronghorn. Historically, they numbered about 15 million individuals. Today, there are fewer than 1 million. This quintessential American athlete (they go by the scientific name, *Antilocapra americana,* after all) is the fastest land mammal in our hemisphere and deserves a secure future.

Another important part of the effort to bring back the American Serengeti involves grassland breeding birds. Birds that breed in the Great Plains are the most rapidly and consistently declining suites of birds in North America. Declining grassland birds include the mountain plover, long-billed curlew, lark bunting, lesser prairie-chicken, loggerhead shrike, chestnut-collared longspur, and short-eared owl, all of which occur in SPLT's focus area and would benefit from our preserves.

Even the abundant and common creatures—coyote and mule deer are good examples—merit places where they can participate in the natural rhythms of their prey or predator lifestyles, without human interference. Quite simply, they deserve the space to be their beautiful selves.

The Future Of The Southern Plains

Not for a minute do we think our refuges exist in a vacuum. SPLT respects our neighbors' property rights and expects (and usually receives) the same in return. SPLT's setting is in the heart of the Dust Bowl. Our acquisitions are made possible, and provide significant ecological "bang for the buck," due to low land prices and large tracts of intact habitat for sale. The underlying drivers are what Frank and Deborah Popper pointed out decades ago in their call for a "Buffalo Commons."

Out-migration of younger generations, a declining population, and an economy in need of diversification are recognized as the region's top problems. Population decline has resulted in frontier-era human population densities of 2-6 people per square mile across much of the region; and the poverty rate in one of the counties where SPLT works is triple the state average.

When the Poppers first set forward their idea of a Buffalo Commons, Kansas Governor Mike Hayden was a staunch critic. Later sharing the stage with the Poppers, the former governor stated, "I am here to say, 17 years later, that I was wrong."[1] How refreshing is that—a politician that unequivocally apologizes? He went on to say, "Seventeen years ago we wondered what a couple of interlopers from Rutgers know about the High Plains. Not only did what Frank and Deborah predict come true, but the truth is that the out-migration of the Great Plains has been even stronger than they predicted."

Across the plains right now, in an area that seems resistant to change, the undeniable demographic and economic trends are leading to more and more conversations about the need for something new. One promising effort is the Great Plains Ecotourism Coalition, the members of which (SPLT included) believe that the natural beauty of this place is a resource that local economies can bank on. It is SPLT's view that a restoration economy can take root, where visitors stream to the area for the pure joy of planting trees along prairie streams and tearing out fences that are hazardous to wildlife, guided by the vision of an American Serengeti. In the process, those visitors will spend money at local gas stations, motels, and restaurants, thus breathing life into small towns whose main streets are presently lined with shuttered businesses.

SPLT's approach does not entail a large-scale public park managed by government agencies, but rather a network of large private wildlife preserves managed by our organization, which has an unwavering commitment to the preservation of biodiversity. We establish those preserves in the most straightforward and reasonable way: by purchasing land from willing sellers. Our neighbors are free to manage their land for cattle; we'll manage ours for bison and prairie dogs. In fact, we view our private lands conservation solution as completely in step with a region known for its preference for limited government and libertarianism. In short, we're as American as pronghorn.

Expanding SPLT's Preserve Network

Time and time again, the shortgrass prairie offers up more treasures. Visiting scientists find rare plants and animals on our properties, often improving the state of knowledge (for example, the known range, population size, and habitat preference) for these species. A notable example is the Colorado green gentian, a beautiful wildflower found in southeastern Colorado and nowhere else on the planet. SPLT's properties boast some of the largest populations of this plant in existence.

We've seen prairie dogs come surging back from plague on our preserves because we've taken away the other threats—shooting and poisoning—that prevent recovery elsewhere. Our area also has a particularly high density of burrowing owls, no doubt because of the large prairie dog complexes that remain. This pint-sized owl is active during the day and, in our region, breeds and raises its young within prairie dog burrows.

Other wildlife that find refuge on SPLT preserves include elk, pronghorn, mule deer, coyote, badger, bobcat, golden eagles and hawks, songbirds, and many others. The region experiences a fascinating phenomenon each fall: the large, charismatic, and long-lived tarantula can be seen crossing the prairie en masse to breed and create new generations.

As a result of shallow seas during the Cretaceous Age, marine fossils are found in abundance, including countless clams,

15

ammonites, and mussels, as well as occasional shark-teeth, the latter reminding visitors that large sharks once swam through what is now an ocean of grass.

Our preserves all have unique conservation values well worth preserving. But we're not about to stop expanding our preserve network. With E.O. Wilson's words ringing in our ears, SPLT will continue to acquire more land because more land means more refuge for more wildlife. We have another $1 million to raise to complete our expansion of Heartland Ranch to 18,000 acres. We've given ourselves 2019 to do it so that we can quickly pivot to other opportunities to expand our existing preserves and establish new ones. Please consider supporting SPLT's effort for a new, wilder west and check out our latest progress report on our website southernplains.org.[2] We deliberately keep our overhead low so that we can convert donor dollars into land: fully protected, permanently preserved, land, and all the wildlife within.

---

1 https://news.rutgers.edu/feature-focus/recent-census-data-validate-professor's-contentious-'buffalo-commons'-plan/20091029#.XCAfLC2ZM_N
2 https://southernplains.org/wp-content/uploads/2018/11/SPLT-Progress-Report-Fall-2018.pdf

FILLING THE ARC OF APPALACHIA: RESTORING WILDNESS TO SOUTHERN OHIO

BY NANCY STRANAHAN, DIRECTOR,
ARC OF APPALACHIA

This is the improbable story of how the Arc of Appalachia Preserve System came to be. It all started back in 1995, when my husband and I set out to raise money to save a dying but botanically significant 60-acre 1930-era cave tourist enterprise in southern Ohio from subdivision and development. Our attempts attracted showers of well-meaning counsel from friends and colleagues. Not all were encouraging. "That will never work." "We love your enthusiasm but..." "You know you can't do this without a professional fund-raising plan, right?" "What are you going to do with the donations if you fail?"

We were further intimidated by the specter of the thwarted attempts of people *much* more well-connected, knowledgeable, and well-funded than ourselves. One such luminary was our heroine, the late Dr. Lucy Braun, 20th-century Cincinnati botanist and champion of the Great Eastern Forest.[1] When Lucy mobilized to save one of the last old-growth forests that lay across the Ohio River in nearby Kentucky, the trees were felled despite her best efforts. Who did we think we were?

From our viewpoint, we were just common everyday people who were running a small retail bakery and gift shop in a city market in downtown Columbus. On one hand we were, admittedly, decent naturalists, but weighing heavily on the other end of the scale were the facts that our financial resources were modest, we didn't have a clue how to go about fund-raising, we were flaming introverts, and we were heavily preoccupied by our 60-plus hour work week that began at 3:00 am each morning.

"What in heaven's name were we thinking?"

Recalling those days, it wasn't boldness or misplaced confidence that ignited our drive. It was desperation. We were old enough to have seen the sustainability dreams of the 1960s and 70s long past dashed. Anguish over the future of our world and everything we most loved about it smoldered on the edge of our consciousness. The ache could only be kept at bay by staying fiercely busy.

Furthermore, we had just returned from our first trip out of country to South and Central America. En route to the Amazon, we flew over thousands of acres of burning rainforest in Brazil. In Belize, we stood on the shore of entire bays filled with floating plastic. Yet in these same locales we tasted—for the first time in our lives—the intoxicating nectar of tropical biodiversity.

An unnamed hole that had been yawning in my soul for my entire life was suddenly and astonishingly filled—filled by the whoops of howler monkeys greeting the dawn, jaguar prints padding across a pristine beach, dozens of screaming parrots flying across a setting sun, and the gentle breeze of vampire bat wings against my face at night—thankfully just on the other side of my mosquito netting! In the frenzied vortex of life that swirls in an intact tropical rainforest, I was no longer a disconnected and disenfranchised observer of nature. I belonged.

I left the jungle transformed. I had a name for my pain, and best of all, I now knew the remedy. Returning home, I could no longer justify the self-serving "someday-I'll-just-escape-to-a-cabin-in-the-woods" fantasy that had previously propped my daily labors. I passionately knew I needed to dedicate my life to

No culture recognized the significance of Ohio's rich flora and fauna better than the Hopewell Culture that occupied the region 2,000 years ago and built Junction Earthworks. © Tim Anderson, Jr.

protecting wildlands and biodiversity. I *could* try to learn Spanish and live in a Volkswagen van in Costa Rica. But I would likely end up accomplishing nothing of significance (plus I'm lousy at languages and engine repair).

Or, I *could* work in my own homeland of Ohio, the very place I always dreamed of escaping. Here I knew the language, understood the natural history, and had wide and well-established social networks. Not to mention the fact that Ohio certainly needed all the help it could get!

I was afire with a cause looking for a project, and it wasn't long before a project found me. In an attempt to save the significant geological and biological features of the cave park known as *7 Caves*, my husband and I founded a new non-profit called *The Highlands Nature Sanctuary*.[2] The new nature preserve took its first tentative breath in the world with no acres of land to its name and no assets in the bank.

Looking back through the two decades that followed, and recounting the many events, people, and synchronicities that transformed the Highlands Nature Sanctuary into the Arc of Appalachia Preserve System it is today, I have to say those prudent early counselors were right. It *shouldn't* have worked. But it did, and it worked beyond our wildest dreams! Today the Highlands Nature Sanctuary is nearly 3,000 acres in size, composed of 68 separate land acquisitions. Astonishingly, the Sanctuary is now just one of 22 preserves scattered across southern Ohio. The Arc of Appalachia Preserve System, as it stands today, is more than 7,000 acres in size and represents 17 million in acquisition dollars.

No, none of this *should* have worked out this way. The how and the why it did is the subject of this article, at least to the degree that the story can be told. Unexplainable are the miracles and the saved-in-the-nick-of-time dramas that consistently accompanied our evolution. *There were so many of them!* But what I *can* describe are some of the landing pads we built to receive those miracles.

Admittedly, it's intimidating to try to tell the story of the Arc of Appalachia in the context of so many stellar conservation projects, much larger than ours, that have taken place across the United States. Ohio doesn't boast the mountains of Colorado, the big ranch lands of California, the estuaries of Panhandle Florida, or the vast timberlands of Maine. Ohio is one of the most populated states in the nation (7th), one of the most densely populated (10th), and THE most polluted (#1). It has one of the lowest percentages of federally protected land (9th), and a land use that is high in both industry and agriculture. Yet, perhaps, these are the *very elements* that make this story worthy of being told around the campfire. Perhaps the value of this tale is the simple demonstration that: "If it can be done in Ohio, it can be done anywhere." And *anywhere and everywhere* is exactly where our country's preservation work needs to be done.

How To Preserve Land In Ohio
8 Principles That Guided The Arc Of Appalachia

#1 Romance The Land

Saving private land, of course, always comes down to finding the funds to do it. Here at the Arc of Appalachia, although we have been substantially aided by grants over the years, the true power of our organization lies in our private benefactors. People will save what they love. Practically speaking, this means someone has to romance our property campaign to our far-flung donors.

Here in Ohio, as in every other state, there is *much* that is easy to love. The mixed mesophytic forest is a particularly rich ecoregion in the larger Eastern Deciduous Forest, occupying a narrow corridor along the western foothills of the Appalachian Mountains that begins in Alabama and moves northward into southwestern Pennsylvania. As the mixed mesophytic forest approaches Kentucky, it widens dramatically to take in most of West Virginia and a large swath of land across southern and eastern Ohio. This mixed mesophytic forest ecoregion boasts exceptional temperate terrestrial biodiversity, from songbirds to snails to salamanders, as well as extravagant freshwater aquatic diversity. Consequently, Ohio, Kentucky, and West Virginia are some of the best places *in the world* to preserve the Temperate Deciduous Forest Biome, considered by ecologists to be one of the most disturbed of Earth's biomes and therefore deeply worthy of protection.

Ohio has significant physiographic features, including Lake Erie to the north and the beautiful Ohio River to the south. In the northwest corner of the state are the remnants of the Great Black Swamp. The karst landscapes of southwestern Ohio boast some of the most spectacular wildflower displays in all of the eastern United States. Also in the southwest quadrant are rare, unglaciated, eastern prairie ecosystems that shelter dozens of endangered and threatened wildflowers. The most dissected of Ohio's Appalachian foothills—known as the *Little Smokies of Ohio*—are located in southcentral Ohio. Some of Ohio's most spectacular rock shelters, cliffs and recess caves can be found in the Hocking Hills region of southeastern Ohio.

Our work acknowledges that Ohio *IS* beautiful. Here at the Arc, our staff and board members fall in love with every parcel we hope to buy *before* we craft our public campaign, risking the heartbreak of failure in the process, but infusing our campaign with passion, enthusiasm, and commitment.

#2 Honor Indigenous Roots

No culture recognized the significance of Ohio's rich flora and fauna better than the Hopewell Culture that occupied the region 2,000 years ago. These American Indians built massive earthwork and mound complexes almost exclusively in southern

Ohio—36 complex monuments in total. Some were so large they could be measured in square miles; several were astronomically aligned with major celestial events. The great earthen walls and mounds engineered by the Hopewell Culture—along with ceremonial art that captured the spiritual essence of Ohio's native animals—artistically represent Ohio's greatest cultural florescence *ever*.

The Arc of Appalachia has played a pivotal role in buying and saving four of these great earthen complexes—deliberately embedding them within large protected natural areas. We have found that fund-raising projects involving both natural and historical preservation have been the most compelling campaigns in our entire history. No two fund-raising drives have been more successful, nor heady, than our last minute campaigns to buy Junction Earthworks[3] and Spruce Hill Earthworks[4] off the auction block.

If we are to undertake the task of nature preservation, here at the Arc we believe it is essential to honor the people who cared for the land long before we did.

#3 Reject All Fund-Raising Advice

If it were a cookie-cutter process to raise money for a good cause, all non-profits would be well funded. Fortuitously, we decided early on that if we were to succeed in fund-raising, we had to take the path less traveled.

Perhaps of greatest importance is what we decided NOT to do. We didn't print t-shirts, send out multiple mailings a year, nor issue credit cards. We didn't sell calendars, tote bags, or ball caps. We didn't sell bricks with donors' names on them, nor print the names of our benefactors in our annual news magazine. We didn't host silent auctions or high-ticket dinners. We've never phoned donors to ask for a donation. We've never used guilt or anxiety to solicit a donation, nor have we manufactured preservation crises that didn't really exist. We don't sell or buy mailing lists.

We wouldn't think of doing background checks on our donors' finances. We don't concoct cleverly named giving levels and then urge donors to climb to the next highest level with each passing year. We have never hired or contracted marketing experts. We think every committed Arc employee and every board member performing his or her role with excellence is the best fundraising strategy ever.

In summary, we treat our donors like the brilliant, worldly, and sophisticated people they are. We believe the best strategy to serve our donors is to perform our mission prudently, creatively, and efficiently. We ask our donors to support the Arc of Appalachia with just one donation a year. The space on the donation form asking donors for the amount they wish to give is a blank line.

Even though only a very small minority of people in Ohio love nature enough to volunteer or write a check for land preservation, those who do are actively seeking out effective nonprofits to accomplish their most heartfelt goals. Once they gain trust in an organization, we have found they give with *astonishing* self-sacrifice and generosity. Here at the Arc, we are blessed to work with some of the finest, most enlightened, and passionate people on the planet.

#4 Believe In The People

We believe non-profits are like any other natural community. Our health and sustainability depend on the quality and diversity of our relationships. And so, we invest in our own species. We bank on the premise that our human capacity to destroy is surpassed only by our capacity to love and regenerate.

We practice nonjudgement. We look for magic in every new person we meet. Greeting each new acquaintance, we ask, "Who are you, and what new creative endeavor might we do together?" A non-profit is never short on money—only people.

We trust in people's inscrutable impulses to work in collaboration, even when they are living miles apart and are completely unknown to each other. Just as distantly spaced trees are connected and nourished by an invisible network of mycelia, our many miracles have demonstrated that people of good will are invisibly connected by forces more mysterious and powerful than we will ever know.

We are willing to let go of control. "Step back and make room for the magic."

#5 Donors Are Like Family—Keep Them Informed

Perhaps the Arc of Appalachia's greatest quality is the extent to which our staff, donors, board members, and volunteers feel like one big family. Like any healthy family, connection relies on good communication, which is accomplished through the usual social network venues, a large and festive annual gathering, and the yearly publishing of a plump, full color magazine.

The news magazine is perhaps the most important thing we do to drive our organization forward. This yearly publication unleashes the full power of story—relaying vivid, personal accounts of our campaign properties. In the storytelling process, we impart to our readers a deep knowledge of the lands we are trying to buy—their natural history, beauty, regional significance, and singularity—accompanied with detailed maps. Through these essays our donors become nearly as deeply informed about our land projects as are staff and board members. When donors become this knowledgeable, the quality of the ideas they contribute to our organization is astonishing. Together our board, volunteers, staff, and donors become a tightly knit, unified team.

#6 Fraternize With Artists

Just as the Arc of Appalachia's land stewardship practices are based on science, and our financial management on sound accounting principles, our land preservation efforts rest on ethics and compassion. Thus our annual magazine not only addresses the rational mind, but speaks to the heart—communicating through the creative works of photographers, painters, and poets. With the help of these artists, our magazine is not just informative, but stunningly beautiful and uplifting.

Our fraternization doesn't stop with the news magazine. Each year the Arc offers residency to a number of artists in our overnight facilities, and we host several creative art & nature collaborations.

#7 Stay Agile—Master Plans Are To Meant To Be Broken

The Arc of Appalachia is opportunistic and responsive. Our special nonprofit niche is our ability to respond quickly to land acquisition emergencies. Our board has the ability to communicate rapidly and pass a resolution in 24-48 hours when pressed to do so. And, although we have land-buying priorities and three-year strategic plan, we perceive them as guides—not walls. We can completely veer off our best-laid plans whenever an unexpected but compelling land opportunity presents itself.

The 22 nature preserves that the Arc of Appalachia has acquired and assembled over the years are exceptionally beautiful and biodiverse. Most of them were unplanned. Collectively they are grander than any rational plan we could have ever crafted.

#8 Give Back

A person who only takes and never gives back will eventually exhaust and repel his or her colleagues and friends. Similarly, it behooves a nonprofit to not only focus on serving its inner community of volunteers and donors, but to give back to the larger world with services the larger world values. To this purpose the Arc of Appalachia dedicates substantial resources to the management of more than 40 miles of hiking trails, guided hikes, special events, and three educational museums—all of which are free to the public. Also offered to the public are cabin and group lodge rentals, guided retreats, and intensive nature education courses.

Why Do Some Of Us Love Biodiversity So Much & Why Is It Worth Saving?

Not everyone loves Life in all of its magical multiplicity. Those who deeply cherish Life in *all* its forms have a special sensitivity to the tension that exists between separateness and unity. On one hand, we celebrate biodiversity; on the other, the Oneness of all Life. Parents love a newborn baby because they feel the child is an extension of themselves. We love the sandhill crane and the spotted salamander for the same reason. When we find a piece of ourselves in every living thing, we naturally want to protect every holy embodiment of Life, in all of its splendid diversity.

Buying back the land to preserve biodiversity is heady stuff. With every acre saved, there will be more tree frogs chanting in June, more wood thrushes filling the valleys with flute music, more crickets and katydids turning leaves into late summer song, more wildflowers to grace our earth. Chances are life on Earth is *not* like the Titanic, either sailing or sinking. It is more like floating on an ocean in a life raft that keeps crumbling away at its edges, losing species with every roll of the wave.

Here at the Arc it pleases us to no end to help make that raft as large and complex, as strong and biodiverse, as beautiful and inclusive, as our hands, hearts, and dollars can accomplish.

For more information, or to support the Arc of Appalachia, please see our website at arcofappalachia.org where you will see a listing of our current land acquisition projects. At the time of this writing (February 2019), we are working on adding another 940 acres of natural areas to the Arc of Appalachia Preserve System. If

1 https://cincymuseum.org/dr-e-lucy-braun/
2 http://arcofappalachia.org/highlands-nature-sanctuary/
3 http://arcofappalachia.org/junction-earthworks/
4 https://www.nps.gov/hocu/learn/historyculture/spruce-hill-earthworks.htm

SAFEGUARDING AN ADIRONDACK WILDLIFE CORRIDOR, FOR WILDLIFE AND PEOPLE

BY JON LEIBOWITZ, EXECUTIVE DIRECTOR OF NORTHEAST WILDERNESS TRUST

There is a place on the western shore of Lake Champlain where forest still dominates the landscape and bobcats, bear, otters, and mink can still wander from the lake to the Adirondack High Peaks through rocky hills and along river corridors.

Stemming from Split Rock Wild Forest, the largest expanse of protected and undeveloped Lake Champlain shoreline in New York, Split Rock Wildway follows the waterways and forests of the West Champlain Hills that lie between and alongside rich farmland in the Champlain Valley. It sneaks tenuously under and across Interstate Highway 87 and slips quietly past scattered development. The Wildway links two critical ecosystems—the fertile lowlands of the Champlain Valley with the rugged High Peaks to the west—to provide a natural pathway for both wildlife and people.

The vision to fully protect Split Rock Wildway involves securing a roughly 20-mile corridor and within that distance, the permanent protection of about 15,000 acres. To date, at least, 7,000 acres have been secured by the New York Department of Environmental Conservation, the Northeast Wilderness Trust and our partners at the Eddy Foundation (theeddy.org), Open

Space Institute (openspaceinstitute.org), Adirondack Land Trust (adirondacklandtrust.org), and Champlain Area Trails (champlainareatrails.com). Acre-by-acre and property-by-property, this number continues to grow.

The idea of connecting Lake Champlain to the interior of the Adirondacks is part of a global conservation trend in recognizing the threat of fragmentation, as confirmed by studies of island biogeography, along with the counter opportunity of focusing on connectivity and wildlife corridors. Likewise, out of the original idea of Split Rock Wildway, a larger effort to connect the lake to the mountains has taken hold in New York.

A key part of the broader lake to peaks link is the proposed Eagle Mountain Preserve. At more than 2,400 acres, and sitting between two large conservation blocks, the property is quintessential Adirondack wildland. This strategically located parcel represents an opportunity to conserve landscape-scale wilderness in an area underrepresented by conserved lands within New York's Adirondack Park. Conifer-fringed ponds dot the landscape, peregrine falcons nest on its cliffs, and mother bears raise their young among the rapidly rewilding forests. This densely forested property consists primarily of northern hardwood and conifer forests, with patches of cliff & talus, miles of clear running brooks, and many vernal pools and seepage wetlands. Seepage wetlands thaw first in the spring and provide some of the earliest browse for energy strapped wildlife (such as bear, moose, and deer—all present on the property) at the end of a long winter.

With the reality of anthropogenic climate change, climate resiliency is now recognized as being critically important to conservation strategies. For land to act as a long-term corridor, the property must also be able to withstand the worst of climate change. On this front, Eagle Mountain ranks as 'Far Above Average' for its climate resiliency, according to The Nature Conservancy's 'Resilient and Connected Landscape' dataset.[1] Resilient sites like

Northeast Wilderness Trust's Eagle Mountain project will lengthen and strengthen Split Rock Wildway and safeguard ponds, wetlands, and streams. © Brendan Wiltse

Eagle Mountain are defined as having "sufficient variability and microclimate options to enable species and ecosystems to persist in the face of climate change and which will maintain this ability over time." This means that long into the future, Eagle Mountain Preserve, if protected, will serve wildlife well.

Like much of New York and New England, Eagle Mountain has seen its share of logging. However, also like much of the Northern Forest, the property has shown a tenacious ability to rebound and rewild. To help Northeast Wilderness Trust secure Eagle Mountain and continue adding to the protected lands of Split Rock Wildway, please go to our website, newildernesstrust. org.

The Northeast Wilderness Trust was founded in 2002 by a group of conservationists to fill an open niche in the regional conservation community. At the time, many local land trusts focused on open space protection, and some regional groups effectively conserved farmlands and managed timberlands, but no regional land trust focused exclusively on protecting wilderness areas. With a committed board, professional staff, and clear mission, the Northeast Wilderness Trust has been remarkably effective for a small organization filling a unique niche, conserving more than 10,000 acres in its first ten years. The trust now protects more than 26,000 acres of wilderness in Maine, Massachusetts, New Hampshire, Vermont, New York, and Connecticut.

---

1 http://www.conservationgateway.org/ConservationByGeography/NorthAmerica/ UnitedStates/edc/reportsdata/terrestrial/resilience/Pages/default.aspx

REWILDING ARGENTINA AND BEYOND: PARK BY PARK

BY SOFIA HEINONEN AND LUCILA MASERA, CONSERVATION LAND TRUST ARGENTINA

Wildlands explorer and philanthropist Doug Tompkins, who'd made his fortune by founding The North Face and Esprit, started buying and saving wildlands in southern Chile three decades ago, and accelerated his pace of land conservation after marrying Kris McDivitt Tompkins, former CEO of the outdoor company Patagonia. They soon were invited to Argentina to help save land there, too. To date, Tompkins Conservation and partners have secured more than 2 million acres of wild lands and waters and helped establish or expand dozens of parks in Chile and Argentina

As Doug Tompkins, who tragically died in a kayak accident two years ago, liked to say: *Large, intact, ecologically vibrant landscapes are sources of inspiration, beauty, and economic vitality for human societies, as well as the home to our wild neighbors in the community of life.*

Tompkins Conservation is the umbrella name for a diverse range of conservation initiatives founded by Kristine and Douglas Tompkins to create national parks, sustain biodiversity, restore degraded lands, reintroduce missing species, and encourage environmental activism. In Argentina, Tompkins Conservation works through two entities: the Conservation Land Trust Argentina (CLT) and Fundación Flora y Fauna Argentina (FFyFA), which share the same vision and mission and work in close cooperation on several projects in Argentina.

Vision

Our vision is flourishing ecosystems where natural processes operate freely and all native species thrive in perpetuity. Lands used to produce resources for people are used with care, supporting local traditions. Large, interconnected, and representative protected areas including national parks attract large numbers of human visitors to experience their beauty and wildlife—and thus human communities recognize Nature as their main source of prosperity and well-being.

Mission

Our mission is to establish new parks, help restore and rewild landscapes and marine ecosystems, promote direct benefits to rural communities, and foster a culture of activism—in which people love and defend the wild world. By 2026 we hope to have created at least ten new national parks covering 5 million acres (2 million hectares) of tropical, subtropical, and temperate habitat on land and sea. These parks would benefit more than 15 rural communities and 200,000 people, and have global value as arks of biodiversity and storehouses of naturally sequestered carbon.

Values

Sharing The World With Other Creatures:

We consider that both human and nonhuman life on Earth have value in themselves and should be cared for equally.

Tompkins Conservation biologists and colleagues have been systematically restoring missing species to Iberá. The ultimate rewilding goal is restoration of the top carnivores, including Jaguar. © Matias Rebak

Beauty As A Basic:

We believe that beauty is a value that is intrinsic to all living things. It is not a mere sentimental and idiosyncratic human effect, but our way to describe our encounters with vitality, life affirmative patterns and relationships; it is our shorthand for those experiences that exceed survival and enable us to flourish.

Public Spaces:

We believe in the role of governments to safeguard parks and wilderness areas so that they retain their ecological values and can be visited by local and global citizens.

Constant Action And Commitment:

We believe in the proactive care of natural ecosystems— to restore habitats, reintroduce missing species, and promote a culture of activism so that defenders arise against those who seek to destroy public goods for the benefit of a few, and empowered local groups benefit from their region's natural heritage.

Eco-Localism:

We believe that committed citizens can build the next economy on a regional level around national parks, by working on regenerative production. By achieving conservation as a consequence of production, rural communities can promote well-being and local pride.

Achievements In Argentina

1992. Douglas Tompkins creates the Conservation Land Trust (CLT) and begins working on large-scale conservation projects in South America.

1997. CLT begins its first project in Argentina by purchasing

Estancia San Alonso, a cattle ranch in the middle of the Iberá wetlands. In the subsequent decade, CLT purchases almost 350,000 acres (142.000 hectares) for conservation and grassland restoration in the area.

2004. Monte León National Park is created in Santa Cruz province as result of a large land donation by CLT and its sister organization Conservacion Patagonica.

2007. CLT's rewilding team reintroduces giant anteaters to Iberá. Today there are more than 100 individuals living in the wild. This project is followed by the reintroduction of pampas deer, lowland tapirs, collared peccaries, and green-winged macaws.

2009. Iberá Provincial Park is created, protecting 1,358,500 acres (550,000 hectares).

2014. The property El Rincon is donated to enlarge Perito Moreno National Park.

2014. Impenetrable National Park is created in Chaco province as result of grassroots advocacy and a lead private donation from CLT.

2015. Patagonia National Park is created in Santa Cruz to include lands donated by CLT and its sister organization Fundación Flora y Fauna Argentina. The first jaguar arrives in Iberá Park after half a century of absence in the region.

2016. CLT donates lands in the Iberá wetlands to the Argentinean government to establish Iberá National Park.

2017. A bill to create the first two marine national parks in the Argentine Sea is presented in Congress.

In numbers, these achievements in Argentina add up to 5 new parks; 1,056,000 more protected acres, and 250 individuals of 6 reintroduced species.

Working With Our Hearts And Heads

We are a group of conservationists from different regions and professions, united by our love for wildlands and the people who live around them. Since 1997, the Conservation Land Trust Argentina has been building one of the most experienced teams in Latin America focused on creating national parks, wildlife conservation and rewilding, establishing ecotourism destinations, training conservation advocates, and working with local entrepreneurs interested in wildlife-oriented development. Most CLT staff live at the parks we help create, interacting with authorities and local stakeholders, as well as with the wildlife that is at home in these protected areas.

Additionally we have a national management team, mostly based in Buenos Aires, focused on communication, institutional and political relations, legal aspects related to the establishment and management of protected areas, activism campaigns, land transactions, and finance.

Why Argentina?

Argentina is the eighth largest country in the world, its territory extending from the Tropics to Antarctica, and from vast plains to the highest peaks in South America. As a result, the country hosts a great diversity of natural environments: rainy jungles, cloudy forests, wetlands, savannas and tropical grasslands, deserts, prairies, steppes, coastal wetlands, ice fields, and one of the most productive seas on Earth.

Argentina has perhaps the best national park service in Latin America and a society that supports conservation. The country's primarily urban population favors the continued existence of great wild areas with low human density.

Additionally, President Mauricio Macri's administration has a publicly stated goal of doubling the surface covered by the country's national parks and is taking bold actions toward this objective. In the last two years, the national government enlarged the Natural Reserve Otamendi, Perito Moreno National Park, and Patagonia National Park, and created Pinas, Aconquija, and Iberá

National Parks and the Natural Reserve Isla de los Estados. It also expanded the national park network toward the Argentine Sea, creating a new category of "marine national parks;" currently there is a bill in Congress to establish the first two—Yaganes and Burdwood Bank II National Parks.

Full Nature: Building The Bridge Between Ecology And Economy

After more than 15 years working in Argentina, the Conservation Land Trust developed our own model to help advance into the next economy through the creation of national parks that become economic engines for local communities. We named it "Full Nature" and it seeks to build a new territorial model where large national parks with their full ecological components become ecotourism destinations. The result is local economic vitality, local pride, and cultural continuity in neighboring communities.

National parks, "one of the greatest expressions of democracy," as Doug Tompkins often said, represent the gold-standard of conservation and sustainable use of natural ecosystems. They are public spaces open to visitation by all the world citizens and have a strong legal status that guarantees they last for the long term. As Doug put it, "National parks have a lot of benefits. One of them is that they get people out into Nature. They disregard one's socioeconomic status. They represent a good form of social equity. They belong to everyone."

Complete Ecosystems — Rewilding

Through rewilding—helping ecological processes and missing species return to degraded landscapes—national parks and other protected areas achieve their maximum natural expression. Through various techniques, including reintroducing wildlife, an active program of rewilding can heal the wounds caused by unsustainable human activities and help protect imperiled species.

Ecotourism — Territorial Brand

When parks exude beauty and natural vitality, especially through the spectacle of abundant and easy-to-see wildlife, an ecotourism destination can be established to promote a new economy for neighboring communities. At CLT we work to make our national park projects into territorial brands, which encourages large-scale and regulated visitation bringing new economic potential to these regions.

Community Development

The creation of a territorial brand and ecotourism destination anchored by national parks encourages investment in local communities by public and private development institutions. Thus, rural communities that were previously deprived of adequate public investment and even self-esteem, are incorporated into national and international sustainable development agendas. Our multidimensional program to foster community development is called "Habitat Humanitas."

Projects

Iberá Park

Starting year: 1999
Acquired territory: 341,205 acres / 138,140 hectares
Location: Corrientes Province

Iberá brings together a national protected area with a provincial one, to create the largest park in Argentina, comprising roughly 700,000 total hectares. The center of this great subtropical plain harbors the vast wetlands or "esteros." Around it, a great diversity of natural communities can be found: the alto-parana Atlantic forests, chaco forest, espinal, and open grasslands. Since 1999, the Conservation Land Trust has purchased almost 150,000 hectares and already donated 80,000 to the national government to create the Iberá National Park. The remaining donation is planned for the end of 2018. Additionally, CLT worked to promote the legal protection of 1,358,500 acres (550,000 hectares) of land as a provincial park.

Iberá hosts some go the largest populations in the world of marsh deer and the rare strange-tailed tyrant. These wetlands are home to thousands of capybaras and yacare caimans, while in its grasslands and savanas, greater rheas, southern viscacha, and the mysterious maned wolf thrive.

As a result of CLT's rewilding program, the last years have seen regionally extinct species come back to their original habitat. The anteater, pampas deer, tapir, collared peccary, and spectacular green-winged macaw — the bird had been extinct for around 100 years in the whole country — are helping complete the beauty of this generous land. Hopefully, soon the presence of the authentic king of Iberá, the jaguar, will be felt again.

We have ongoing programs in Iberá for reintroducing almost all the regionally extinct species, including bare-faced curassow and giant otter. At the same time, we work for a thriving regional economy for three rural communities: Carlos Pellegrini, San Miguel, and Concepcion.

El Impenetrable National Park

Starting year: 2014
Acquired territory: 316,000 acres / 128,000 hectares
Location: Chaco Province

The Chaco is the largest dry subtropical forest in the world, shared by Brazil, Paraguay, Bolivia, and Argentina. Most of this ecosystem (62%) is located in Argentina, where it has suffered systematic degradation by intensive logging, forest settlements, cattle grazing, and most significantly by conversion to soybean plantations, which has destroyed hundreds of thousands of hectares. Within the Argentinean Chaco, "La Fidelidad," a 250,000-hectare property located in the provinces of Chaco and Formosa, represents a rare example of chaco forest in excellent condition. In 2014, after the owner of La Fidelidad was murdered, a group of NGOs led by Tompkins Conservation, through Flora y Fauna Argentina, successfully encouraged the creation of El Impenetrable National Park, comprising 130,000 hectares of La Fidelidad property within the Argentinean province of Chaco.

The park is uniquely positioned to conserve ecosystems representative of the Chaco region—including Chaco dry forest, the gallery forest of the Teuco and Bermejito rivers, grasslands, and lagoons—and to act as a development engine for neighboring communities, through an ecotourism-based economy. El Impenetrable National Park supports outstanding biodiversity— including more than 13,000 vascular plant species, more than 400 bird species, and more than 120 mammal species, among them jaguar, giant armadillo, giant anteater, tapir, the endemic Chacoan peccary, and the secretive maned wolf.

The five main towns surrounding La Fidelidad, each with marginal logging and cattle farming as main economic activities, could greatly benefit by the creation of a new ecotourism destination. Local residents maintain cultural values (handicrafts, music, and gastronomy) that are adapted to this harsh environment. These attributes could attract tourists, if well presented.

So far, only half of the projected park has been created. Half of the property is on the northern bank of the Bermejo River, in the province of Formosa. This property is key as it would block the entrance of poachers to the park, who currently have access from the north. Provincial political relations need to be developed in Chaco and Formosa.

Rewilding work here will include reintroduction or augmentation of guanacos, marsh deer, giant otter, jaguar, and other regionally extinct or threatened species. A baseline inventory needs to be done.

Community development will focus on training of local nature and birdwatching guides. Local towns will benefit from entrepreneurs who specialize in river guiding, photographic safari, and wildlife tracking expeditions.

Patagonia National Park

Starting year: 2012
Acquired territory: 316,000 acres / 128,000 hectares
Location: Santa Cruz Province

In July 2014, Patagonia National Park Argentina was created by Congress due to the initiative of three conservation groups, Flora y Fauna Argentina, Aves Argentinas, and Ambiente Sur. We are in the process of purchasing land amounting to 1,195,480 acres (484,000 hectares) toward the border with Chile for the expansion of the existing national park. Ultimately, we aim to create a binational park of 1.9 million acres (770,000 hectares) with a unified management vision between the Chilean and Argentine national park systems. This vision includes a common approach to wildlife conservation, a shared idea of community involvement, and the development of transboundary tourism.

The present Patagonia National Park in Argentina includes part of the Buenos Aires Plateau, an almost uninhabited area of harsh climate and austere beauty, holding the only flatland glacier in South America. The plateau is known as the mythical cradle of the now-extinct Tehuelche people, and contains numerous archeological sites with prehistoric remains and art. The plateau is also the core habitat of the critically endangered hooded grebe: monitoring and recovery programs are being implemented for this rare aquatic bird.

Patagonia National Park is expected to develop into a major tourism destination and economic development tool for four local communities. The future expansion of the park includes an already acquired property that includes a World Heritage site, Cueva de las Manos (Cave of the Hands). Along the Pinturas River, where the cave is located, at least 70 archeological sites are known, recording continuous human presence for more than 8,000 years. A binational tourism circuit should provide a wide range of recreational opportunities with minimal infrastructure in order for visitors to experience a landscape largely untrammeled by humankind.

For Patagonia National Park, we will build a local rewilding team to work on guanaco translocation and install trap cameras to understand puma behavior. This team will also work to eliminate exotic species that threaten the hooded grebe. Community development here will include working with Lago Posadas community, which is isolated and dependent on tourism.

The Patagonia Austral Coastal National Park: A New Opportunity

Location: Chubut Province

In the northern coast of Golfo San Jorge, on the Patagonia coastline, there is a small interjurisdictional marine coastal park called "Patagonia Austral." It is one of the only marine coastal parks in Argentina, and it urgently needs to be enlarged and recategorized into national park status to effectively protect this region of land and sea.

The proposed future Patagonia Austral Coastal National Park would include more than 200 kilometers of irregular coast and more than 60 islands where many migratory birds nest. The terrestrial ecosystems contain representative samples of the Patagonia steppe, with numerous streams and temporary lagoons, which increase locally the diversity of birds and insects.

Of the 16 marine bird species that nest in Argentina, 13 raise their young here, in 21 breeding colonies with 1 to 7 seabird species each, including blue-eyed cormorant, rock cormorant, the endemic Chubut steamer duck, and Olrog's gull, considered to be an internationally threatened species. The sea lion colony on the islands has up to 4,000 individuals, representing around 20% of the total population that inhabits the San Jorge Gulf area. The richness of the area also attracts orcas and dolphins. Guanacos, lesser rheas, Patagonian maras, and armadillos also inhabit this diverse area.

There are at least ten properties in the area that would be feasible to purchase and that together define a core of more than 100,000 hectares of rural land. The area has still not been affected by coastal development, and thus current real estate prices reflect the sheep ranching market. It appears that the properties have their land titles in order, their ecological condition is good, and any degraded areas could be recovered by rewilding efforts.

Our goal here is to enlarge and recategorize the interjurisdictional Patagonia Austral Park, creating a national park that extends at least six miles into the sea and six miles inland. We will work to recover native wildlife species and restore key ecological processes, with special emphasis on intertidal marine ecosystems, in such a way that this park spills wildlife over neighboring areas of Patagonia, sea and land. Community development will include working with the community of Camarones (1,500 inhabitants) to create a next economy in the area.

Binational Vision

Argentina - Chile

We widely promote our active conservation model of "Full Nature" and the role of national parks as economic engines for the next economy. We dream of the South American continent actively modeling this idea. A first step toward this wild dream is to create binational parks and ecotourism circuits that benefit local communities.

The Tompkins Conservation teams in Argentina and Chile are already working toward the creation of a future Patagonia Binational Park. We are promoting local communities' identification with a "Patagonia Binational Circuit." Over the long term we want to achieve an ecotourism binational corridor that runs from Pumalín National Park in Chile's Lakes District south to the national parks in Tierra del Fuego.

Argentina - Brazil

The loss of wildlife occurring in northern Argentina has affected the Atlantic forest in the province of Misiones, bordering Brazil, where many species of large birds and mammals have become regionally extinct during the last century. The green-winged macaw, blue-winged macaw, harpy eagle, bare-faced curassow, Brazilian merganser, and giant otter are among the missing natives.

We propose to carry out an initial rewilding project—to reintroduce green-winged macaws and harpy eagles to Iguazú National Park (Misiones). We will also scout the possibility of acquiring land for conservation next to the existing national park, linking it to a nearby provincial park to maintain an Atlantic Forest Wildway.

Argentina - Bolivia

The province of Salta has three protected areas—Baritú National Park, El Nogalar National Reserve, and Laguna Pintascayo Provincial Park—that conserve a threatened and unique ecosystem, the cloudy forest. These protected areas are close to the border with Bolivia and could serve as a platform to start working toward a binational park. Conservationists should scout the province of Salta and Bolivia's border with Argentina for available conservation properties and study the species that need to be reintroduced.

Marine Program

In 2017, CLT expanded its focus beyond terrestrial parks and began advocating for marine protected areas (MPAs) in Argentina's exclusive economic zone. Since then, we have successfully advocated for the creation of marine national parks as a conservation designation and campaigned for the first two marine national parks in the country to be established in law.

We are developing a campaign to educate the public and policymakers about the proposed Marine Blue Route, which will include four marine-coastal protected areas along the Patagonian coast. This route includes one of the greatest Magellanic penguin colonies and is of great importance for seabirds and mammals.

While individual countries may legally control the waters within their exclusive economic zones, the oceans and the diversity of life they sustain know no borders. And thus we dream to create the first bi-oceanic marine protected area in the world. The Patagonia Bi-Oceanic Corridor would cover the waters from the already announced Cape Horn MPA in Chile to the Burdwood Bank MPA, including the Blue Whale Sanctuary and the future Yaganes MPA in Argentina.

Eventually the Tompkins Conservation marine program will advocate for protecting the high seas, beyond the 200 mile zone of national concern, taking advantage of the international debate about this subject that is being led by the United Nations. The waters beyond Argentine jurisdiction are hotspots for illegal, unreported and unregulated industrial fishing, which is seriously depleting ocean life and health within Argentine territorial waters.

National Rewilding

In short, the Conservation Land Trust is carrying out in northern Argentina the most ambitious project of multi-species reintroduction in South America. After twelve years of experience with reintroducing extirpated wildlife in Iberá, we are certain that this is a great conservation strategy to help degraded ecosystems heal. This is especially true in Argentina, where most protected areas no longer sustain their full complement of native species. Many bird and mammal species have been lost. Thus, we want to escalate rewilding strategy to a national level and create a culture of active ecological restoration across the country and beyond. We need to recover populations of jaguar, pampas deer, guanaco (in northern Argentina), marsh deer, tapir, giant and southern river otters, collared and white-lipped peccaries, south Andean deer, anteater, green-winged macaw, harpy eagle, and bare-faced curassow. To achieve this, we need to strengthen the rewilding team, and we need to keep changing the culture in the public administration, mainly the National Park Administration and the Ministry of Environment, so that they support and pursue proactive conservation efforts.

How You Can Help

First of all, we would love to receive you in our lodge, Rincon del Socorro in Iberá so that you can experience the whole project and fall in love with the place and its wildlife.

To make reservations, please contact ibera@dyt-central.com.ar.

Currently, the Argentine programs are partly financed by different NGOs and private donations. But dreams are still big, so we are looking for new partners to join us in our rewilding work in Argentina. Any donation is helpful and gets us closer to our conservation objectives.

For donations, please contact Lucila Masera at lmasera@gmail.com or Brady@tompkinsconservation.org .

ORIGINAL
ECOSYSTEMS

Kebler Pass Aspens in Autumn. © *Evan Cantor*

EASTERN OLD-GROWTH FORESTS THEN AND NOW

BY ROBERT T. LEVERETT

Following several old-growth forest discoveries in western Massachusetts in the late 1980s and early 1990s, I became involved with *Wild Earth* magazine to search for and report on old-growth remnants in the eastern United States. It was an unlikely role for me, given my unrelated educational path (engineering), but my son Rob and I were finding little pieces of the pre-settlement landscape that were supposed to have disappeared by the middle 1800s. The experts had missed them for lack of a proper search image for old growth in New England, yet there they were, in front of our unbelieving eyes. So in the spring of 1988, Rob put his budding artist talents to work, and I, with pen in hand, wrote an article for the *Woodland Steward* publication of the Massachusetts Forestry Association. The title was something like "Old-Growth Forests in the Cold River and Deerfield River Gorges." The rest is history.

As an outgrowth of Rob's and my discoveries, in 1993 I helped organize the first of a series of eastern old-growth conferences that brought together scientists, forest managers, and environmentalists to explore challenges to the identification and preservation of the East's remaining old growth. We called the gatherings the Ancient Eastern Forest Conference Series. Altogether, we held 10 events, and it was at them that I had the privilege and honor of meeting many distinguished scientists who became my mentors. During that golden era, old-growth discoveries mounted, often in places that had been thoroughly explored.

One of the geographical areas that was supposed to have been ravaged by loggers was the Adirondack Mountains of upstate New York. To the surprise of forest historians of the region, though large areas were cut, a substantial acreage of old growth survived. The Adirondack forests were best chronicled by the late Dr. Barbara McMartin, who, in the 1990s, thoroughly researched their logging history. As a result of Dr. McMartin's work, we are confident that several hundred thousand acres have survived. The exact amount is not known, but it is somewhere between 300,000 and 500,000 acres—the largest old-growth reserves in the East. Following McMartin, Dr. Michael Kudish has taken on the role of the old-growth forest expert of Adirondack Park (and of New York's smaller and more southerly Catskill Park).

In the Adirondacks, the Great Smoky Mountains, Big Reed Pond (Maine), or any of the other old-growth remnants spread from Florida to Maine, and westward to Minnesota, there is an ineffable mystery and magic. Shafts of light penetrating a tall canopy of moss-covered trunks, and illuminating a dense carpet of herbaceous plants below, are suggestive of a world inhabited by hobbits and elves.

Forestry texts had been written decades ago on the successional trajectory of forests from early development to old-growth status. Forest succession models typically start with the simple structure of young forests and follow the process into the increasingly complex ones typical of old growth. However, these models mostly concentrate on the trees, their ages and sizes, as opposed to the aggregate ecosystem with all its many species and processes playing out on different time scales. The traditional storyline that emerged from the early models was one of increasing senescence as tree age progressed beyond economic maturity. As a consequence, timber interests have long promoted

Old-growth sleuths have found many previously undocumented old-growth forest groves in eastern North America in the last few decades, which greatly enhanced our understanding of these rich ecosystems. © Robert "Tree Spirit" Leverett

the notion that old forests are unproductive and disease ridden, although they are more cautious these days with their use of pejorative terms. Today, they often justify harvesting of mature trees by lauding species that thrive in early successional habitat.

However, we now know a lot more about old-growth ecosystems than we did in the 1980s and 1990s. We are coming to understand the complex web of life beneath the ground that connects the trees of the same and different species in supportive relationships. The simplistic picture of how forest systems work, promoted by the timber interests, is finally being challenged in mounting scholarly studies.

If this is the good news, there is also the bad. In recent years our old-growth forests have been assaulted by invasive plants and animals, forest pathogens, drought, hurricanes, and of course, the ever-present threat of development. The hemlock woolly adelgid, emerald ash borer, Asian longhorn beetle, gypsy moth, southern pine beetle, and other pests are hammering our forests. The older trees may be at a disadvantage in this war of insect pests and fungal assassins, but it is not yet clear when a tree's defenses are at their strongest.

As if the above threats weren't enough, a new one has emerged to impact forests, young and old. The new threat has been growing for a decade or more—the ugly specter of biomass harvesting for generating heat and electricity by burning wood. This insidious practice has been declared carbon neutral by politicians who fall prey to the green-sounding talking points of the timber and wood products interests. Let's be honest. Biomass harvesting is NOT carbon neutral.

One of the most challenging debates today involving our old-growth and mature second-growth forests falls in the climate change arena. For years, foresters have maintained that young forests grow faster and therefore sequester more carbon than their older counterparts, which are often depicted as geriatric by age 100. However, recent studies have been turning this self-serving belief of the timber interests on its head. It now appears that the larger, older trees are doing the lion's share of the work.

As for my role, I've been measuring trees with serious intent since the early 1990s, and have managed to position myself on the leading edge of field-based tree-measuring techniques. Over the past year, I've been busy developing charts, tables, and graphs showing how trees in the areas I visit acquire their carbon reserves over time. The following table provides a look at a charismatic species, the eastern white pine. The tree being profiled below exemplifies over a dozen that I routinely measure in western Massachusetts.

Growth Profile Of A High Performing White Pine, Mohawk Trail State Forest

Age -yrs	Cir- cum- fer- ence -ft	Trunk Area -ft²	Height -ft	Trunk Form Fac- tor	Trunk Vol- ume -ft³	Abso- lute Gain During Period -ft³	Per- cent- age Gain During Period
25	3.00	0.72	45.00	0.33	10.73	10.73	
50	6.00	2.86	100.00	0.34	97.40	86.67	807.57
100	8.25	5.42	135.00	0.35	255.92	158.51	162.74
150	10.00	7.96	150.00	0.38	453.59	197.67	77.24
200	11.00	9.63	165.00	0.40	635.51	181.91	40.11

I won't go into an explanation of how the above numbers were derived, but they tell the story of the gain in volume in this hypothetical pine's trunk from seedling to an age of 200 years. These volumes can be translated into elemental carbon and the equivalent in terms of CO_2. So where's the controversy? Lumbermen will likely point to the last column in making their argument that the pine's fast growth occurs in the first 50 years.

An increase in volume of 807% from age 25 to age 50 is hard to argue with. Doesn't that prove their case? Not really. Look at the column entitled 'Absolute gain during period – ft^3'. The largest 50-year volume gain is between 100 and 150 years, and even the gain between 150 and 200 years is over twice what it was in the first 50 years. It is the absolute gains that make the climatic difference.

This crucially important lesson about how growth occurs is lost if we just focus on percentage growth data. What they ignore is that a large percent of a very small number can still be a small number. The big pines are the ones possessing a large surface area of needles, which is where the photosynthesis takes place.

It is hard for most people, amateur and professional alike, to judge growth for a very large trunk. What appears to be an insignificant addition at breast height, when spread over a large form, becomes significant.

In an era of rapid climate change, the future of eastern old growth is unclear, but there is no disputing its historical importance to species diversity, climate mitigation, and the human spirit. Old-growth forest deserves our best efforts to preserve it and make a pathway to allowing currently mature regrowth forests to become future old growth.

Suggested Readings On Old-Growth Forest In The Eastern Us

- *Eastern Old-Growth Forests: Prospects for Rediscovery and Recovery,* edited by Mary Byrd Davis;
- *Sierra Club Guide to Ancient Forests of the Northeast,* by Bruce Kershner and Robert Leverett;
- *Among the Ancients: Adventures in the Eastern Old-Growth Forest,* by Joan Maloof
- *Nature's Temples: The Complex World of Old-Growth Forests,* by Joan Maloof
- Old Growth Forest Network website, oldgrowthforest.net
- Native Tree Society website, nativetreesociety.org

WORKING TO RESTORE THE AMERICAN CHESTNUT

BY SARA FERN FITZSIMMONS, TACF DIRECTOR OF RESTORATION

The demise of the American chestnut (*Castanea dentata*) has been described as one of the great ecological disasters of current time. Through the first-half of the 20th century, the species was virtually eliminated from the landscape by an Asiatic blight fungus (*Cryphonectria parasitica*) introduced on Japanese chestnut materials imported to the United States in the late 1800s.

The American chestnut was densely populated with a range from Maine to Georgia. The Pennsylvania Blight Commission estimated that more than 25% of the state's hardwoods were American chestnut trees in the early 1900s. In native forests throughout their range, mature chestnuts are storied to have averaged up to five feet in diameter and up to one hundred feet tall. Many specimens of eight to ten feet in diameter were recorded, and there were rumors of trees bigger still.

Due to their abundance and enormous size, the American chestnut once ranked as the most important wildlife plant in the eastern United States. A large American chestnut tree could produce ten bushels or more of nuts. Chestnut mast supported many species indigenous to the eastern United States including: squirrels, wild turkey, white-tailed deer, black bear, raccoon, and grouse, which once depended on chestnuts as a major food source.

Due to the tree's capacity to regenerate from the root collar, the American chestnut continues to survive as an understory or shrub species. The American chestnut is now typically only found as a small stump sprout, rarely reaching more than 20 feet in height. Although the tree has not been put on the threatened and endangered species list because of its relatively numerous population size, the blight fungus usually kills those stems before they can reach sexual maturity, reproduce and/or expand within its native range. We call the species "functionally extinct."

Although millions of sprouts exist throughout the original range, different management strategies, the importation of other exotic and invasive species, and the influence of hungry deer herds, especially in and around urban and suburban areas, all have influenced the capacity of the species to continue surviving simply through re-sprouting.

Importance Of Native Species And Impact On Wildlife

At The American Chestnut Foundation, we often get asked the question: why should we restore the American chestnut? The species has been virtually absent from the Appalachian forest ecosystem for over a century. Why go through all this effort and expense to save it? While it is true that the species has not had a significant effect on the landscape for more than 100 years, restoring it will certainly increase the overall diversity and health of native Appalachian forests.

As most readers know, native plant species are integral to feeding native insects and large herbivores. If we can increase native flora, we can increase the health of native fauna. Unfortunately, we are losing major pieces of our Appalachian megafauna every decade. Now under attack from different pests and diseases are the eastern hemlock, ashes, and American beech. The hope is that the restoration of the American chestnut will not only lead to improved ecosystem health, but also showcase methods and systems that can be used to assist other native tree species in peril.

Restoration Efforts

Efforts underway to restore the American chestnut include traditional breeding methods, simple conservation strategies, methods that reduce the virulence of the blight fungus, and modern genetic transformation techniques. The American Chestnut Foundation (TACF) works with a wide range of partners to combine these strategies for creating self-sustaining, resilient, and disease-resistant American chestnut populations. While the broadest goal is to restore the American chestnut species, TACF focuses on two major objectives: (1) introducing genetic material(s) leading to disease-resistance in the American chestnut, and (2) preserving the genetic heritage of the American chestnut species by planting and grafting native germplasm.

To avoid inbreeding and to maximize inclusion of regionally-adapted genetic complexes, TACF utilizes many different American chestnut trees from multiple locations throughout the eastern United States. Thus, every generation of planting material requires that hundreds to thousands of trees be properly screened and tested. To date, TACF has conserved more than 1,000 sources of American chestnut from across the native range.

Plant pathogens frequently evolve to overcome plant defenses. Although the blight fungus is not known to have overcome the defenses of the numerous Chinese chestnut trees planted in the US, a future "breakdown" of resistance in blight-resistant chestnut trees is possible. To minimize this risk, the more tools in the resistance toolbox that a tree has, the better. Therefore, combining resistance from Asiatic sources, along with that from novel gene constructs such as the oxalate oxidase gene from wheat, will create a more robust and resilient restoration population.

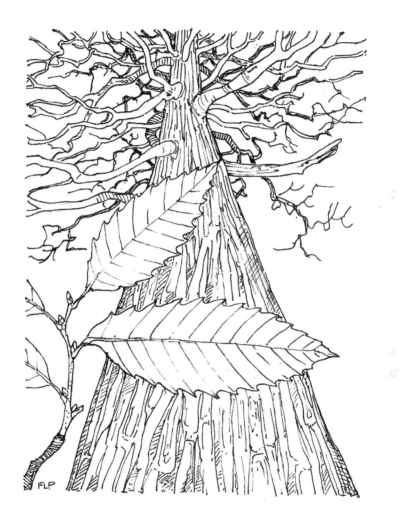

Due to their abundance and enormous size, the American chestnut once ranked as the most important wildlife plant in the eastern United States. © Frederick Paillet.

Many land-owners are interested in receiving blight-resistant American chestnuts that are ready to be used for reforestation. Although that is what TACF is trying to achieve, unfortunately, those materials are not yet available for wide-scale distribution.

Volunteer growers plant trees for conservation, testing, breeding, and demonstration orchards every year. Though potentially blight-resistant American trees are being tested, the work is far from over. Restoration of a native species is the goal. As such, we need as much diversity in our breeding program as possible. As TACF moves forward, it will be vital to incorporate more American chestnuts and different types of breeding strategies to create a self-sustaining American chestnut population for many generations to come.

TACF and its chapters rely on our core of citizen scientists to accomplish many of the breeding activities. Volunteers maintain more than 500 orchards and have planted more than 500,000 trees. There are more than 5,000 members in TACF combining to log some 19,000 hours of volunteer time per year!

How You Can Help

TACF is always looking for new trees for germplasm conservation, places to plant trees, and help in various other field and administrative tasks. To maximize diversity and adaptation of restoration populations, TACF seeks to use as many American chestnut trees as possible.

Starting in 2018, TACF is placing a priority on locating and conserving as many wild American chestnut trees as possible. We need your help to find trees and then collect leaves and/or nuts from them.

1. Go to this website to download a **Tree Locator Form (TLF)** and learn about chestnut identification: acf.org/resources/identification/

2. Download **TreeSnap** on your phone
3. Go for a walk in the woods. Contact your local TACF office to find out if priority areas for scouting have been identified near you.
4. When you find an American chestnut tree
   - **Document** the tree using a TLF or on TreeSnap (or both)
   - AND **Collect a leaf and twig sample** as per the instructions on the TLF
5. **Mail** leaf sample to your nearest TACF office for identification. Include a TLF that is either completed or has your TreeSnap ID on it.

Even if you can't find or plant trees, just joining and spreading the word about chestnut restoration can help continue the work of TACF and its partner organizations to restore more diverse and sustainable forests for the future. For more information about TACF's work, membership options, and other ways to support our efforts, please visit our website at acf.org.

WILDLANDS DEFENSE

Puma symbolizes the restoration of healthy populations of all native species, including top carnivores and other keystone members of our biota, across their native ranges. © Susan Morgan

DECONSTRUCTING TODAY'S GREAT LAND GRAB

BY DAVE FOREMAN

"The plan is to get rid of public lands altogether, turning them over to the states, which can be coerced as the federal government cannot be, and eventually to private ownership.
This is your land we are talking about."

—BERNARD DEVOTO, 1947[1]

In our July chat *Around the Campfire**, I gave a quick introduction and overview of the history and policy of State Trust Lands. In this *Campfire*, I will take on some of the highfalutin assertions made by the hucksters for giving the Federal Public Lands to individual states—the *Land Grab* as Bennie DeVoto wrote in *Harper's* in the 1940s.

As DeVoto wrote 71 years ago, the hard truth is this: if Federal Lands are handed to states, say goodbye to National Forests, National Parks, National Monuments, Wilderness Areas, National Wildlife Refuges, and other public lands where we Americans are free to wander and wonder. To find ourselves and lose ourselves. To have a blissful family picnic or to meet the wild on its own terms. Where we are free to be Americans. Just as we have been for four hundred years. With open land for roving, camping, hunting, fishing, dancing with wolves, howling at the moon....

The big question about the Land Grab of giving the Federal Public Lands to the states is two-part:

1. How much and which of the Federal Public Lands would be given to the states?
2. What state agencies would be given control and management over the transferred lands?

Some other time I'll tackle these questions. Here I want to shoot down the underlying assertions made by the boosters for the Land Grab.

These screwy muddles of history are:

- **The Federal Public Lands should be returned to the states.**
- **Eastern states got a better deal on receiving federal land grants than did western states, which are thereby financially handicapped. That old miscarriage of justice now needs to be righted by giving the Federal Public Lands to the states in which they are found.**
- **Western states are overburdened with high percentages of Federal Public Land.**

Well. First of all, these beliefs are as true as the Easter Bunny laying eggs in your backyard sometime in spring. They are shuck and jive, born in humbug history and self-delusion, traits with which Westerners have always been well blessed. (I am an eighth-generation Westerner, by the way, and the first in my family to have been born off the homestead, so I know something of Westerners.)² These claims are also born in greedy self-interest for some who hope to grab such lands for private gain from the states.

So, let me answer the beliefs and manifestoes of those who call for handing our Federal Public Lands over to the states (another Western trait going back to when Alabama was the West).

Pecos Falls in the original Pecos River Forest Reserve, of 311,040 acres, was one of the first areas withdrawn in January 11, 1892, under the 1891 Forest Protection Act. © Dave Foreman

Myth 1: The Federal Lands Should Be Returned To The States

This outlandish asseveration should be slapped down whenever it comes out of a politician's mouth. The Public Lands were never owned or overseen by the states in any way.[3] Rather, they were tracts of the Public Domain withdrawn from later disposal to railroads, timber barons, homesteaders, and others, and kept for the good of all Americans regardless of where they lived. The Federal Public Domain came into being as soon as such lands were acquired by the United States through conquest, purchase, or treaty.[4] (See Table 1.)

(The lands claimed by European Empires and acquired from them by the United States were overall unsettled. Except, of course, by the towns, pueblos, fields, and hunting grounds of Native American tribes and civilizations. They were not consulted in the imperial game of moving flags around in North America. But this great sin of Manifest Destiny is beyond the scope of this Campfire.)

Table 1: Land Acquisitions To The Public Domain By The United States

Year(s)	Region	Means of Acquisition	Purchase Cost	Acreage
1783	Appalachians to Mississippi River	Treaty of Independence from Great Britain		237 million acres
1802	Louisiana Purchase; Louisiana to Montana	Purchase from France	$23 million	530 million acres
1810-19	Florida	Treaty/Purchase from Spain	$6.7 million	46 million acres
1818	Red River Basin Parts of Minnesota and Dakotas	Treaty with Great Britain		29 million acres
1845	Texas	Bankrupt, Failed Independent Republic Begs to Join US		No Public Domain
1846	Washington, Oregon, Idaho, SW Wyoming, NW Montana	Oregon Compromise with Great Britain		180.6 million acres
1848	California, Nevada, Utah, Colorado, Arizona, New Mexico	Mexican War Conquest and Purchase	$15 million	334.5 million acres5
1850	E New Mexico, bits of Colorado, WY, KS	Purchase from State of Texas	$10 million	78.8 million acres
1853	Southern Arizona, SW New Mexico	Gadsden Purchase from Mexico	$10 million	19 million acres
1867	Alaska	Purchase from Russian Empire	$7.2 million	426 million acres
1898	Hawaii	Conquest of Independent Monarchy		No Public Domain

All of these nearly two billion acres became part of the Federal Public Domain upon acquisition and were managed by the General Land Office in the Department of the Interior. Lands were granted to Revolutionary War veterans, sold to settlers for homesteads, to speculators who sold them to settlers and others, to corporations, timber and mining companies, and were granted to railroad trusts and later to homesteaders.[5] Land was also granted to new states formed within these territorial acquisitions to support public schools and other good things (School Trust Lands).[6] From 1781 to 1976, 1.144 billion acres of the Public Domain were sold or granted to individuals, corporations, and states.[7] None of this Public Domain was ever owned or controlled by a state before it came under federal ownership (except for the 237 million acres east of the Mississippi relinquished by Virginia and other original states from their sprawling land grants from the Crown.)[8] So, no, the Federal Public Lands cannot be returned to states because Federal Public Lands never belonged to states in the first place. Only those suckled on the mother's milk of humbuggery and alternative reality can guilelessly make such an utterance. What is truly being asked by the Land Grabbers is for the people of the whole United States to give up their Federal Public Lands (National Forests, Parks, Monuments, Wildlife Refuges, Wilderness Areas, and other lands) to the sole control of State Trust Land Departments in the states (or maybe to other state agencies).

Myth 2: Eastern States Got A Better Deal On Federal Land Grants Than Did Western States, Which Are Thereby Financially Handicapped. That Old Miscarriage Of Justice Now Needs To Be Righted By Giving The Federal Public Lands To The States In Which They Are Found

Once again, we are here smacked by an assertion that is bassackwards in historical truth. The history of School Trust Land and other grants of Federal Public Land to new states shows that the United States was more generous by far to western states than to those east of the Mississippi River. (See Table 2.) (The original thirteen states and the three states spun off from them—Vermont, Maine, and Kentucky—were not under the Northwest Ordinance and never were part of the Public Domain.)

Table 2: Comparative Federal School Land Grants To States[10]

STATE	ACRES	% of STATE
Ohio	724,000	2.5%
Missouri	1,222,000	2.7%
Wisconsin	982,000	2.3%
Oregon	3,399,360	5.7%
Colorado	3,685,618	5.5%
Idaho	2,963,698	5.5%
Utah	5,844,196	10.7%
Arizona	8,093,156	11%
New Mexico	8,711,324	11.2%

As I wrote in the last *Campfire*, School Trust Land grants to the states grew with time. The states in Table 2 show the three classes of grants to the states: one, two, or four sections in every township. The three dry southwestern states got four school sections because the droughty, rugged landscape was thought to be worth less than the land in earlier states and thus more sections were needed to support schools.

Myth 3: Western States Are Overburdened With Higher Percentages Of Federal Land Than Are Eastern States

It would be better to reword this to say, "Western states are blessed with higher percentages of National Parks, Forests, Wilderness Areas, and such in which to camp, picnic, hike, hunt, fish, and to just get lost from the shackles and stresses of civilization." Moreover, Federal Public Lands protect watersheds (including unsullied mountain snowpacks) for downstream use, clean air, lovely landscapes through which to drive, and good wildlife homes.

However, we need to understand why the eastern states were thickly settled, with nearly every acre being homesteaded or otherwise passed into private ownership, and why so much land in the West was not gobbled up in homesteads. Cleaving the Plains states of the Dakotas, Nebraska, Kansas, and Oklahoma from north to south, the Hundredth Meridian has long been seen as the dividing line between land with enough rainfall to grow crops without irrigation and land without enough rainfall (about twenty inches a year). Roughly, settlers east of the Hundredth Meridian could keep a family on the 160 acres of a homestead while to the west the land was too dry. Moreover, as settlers rode west, they met the Rocky Mountains and later other ranges far too rugged for farming. Not until pioneers and their families made it to Puget

Sound, the Willamette Valley, and coastal valleys of California, did they find well-watered land befitting the kind of farming known east of the Hundredth Meridian. Throughout the Intermountain West, settlement was kept to river valleys and springs and the rest (often called "worthless lands" or "the lands no one wanted") was left unclaimed by homesteaders and stayed in the Public Domain under the General Land Office of the Department of the Interior.⁹

And so, no, the West did not get cheated, but was settled in keeping with the geographical characteristics of the West—aridity and topography (understood by John Wesley Powell nearly 150 years ago). To understand this "tyranny of geography," one need only fly in a window seat from San Francisco to Chicago and look down on Nevada and then on Iowa. The truth of what I write is written on the land.

So. Let's now flip this half-baked snort of the elite Western scoundrels onto its back and ask "Why did the East, Midwest, and South get cheated out of Federal Public Lands which could have become National Forests and National Parks and other Federal Public Land open for picnicking, camping, hiking, hunting, and playing Daniel Boone?"

The answer is the same: rainfall and gentler topography led to the Public Domain east of the Hundredth Meridian being homesteaded, granted, or bought before any tracts could have been withdrawn for National Forests, National Parks, and other federal lands. America east of the Hundredth Meridian was thoroughly settled and taken out of the Public Domain before Yellowstone was withdrawn from settlement and disposal as the first National Park in 1872 or the first Forest Reserves were withdrawn in 1892. It is a national tragedy that the Eastern and Midwestern states were heavily settled before thought of keeping some of the Public Domain was birthed. Think of a Yellowstone-sized National Park in the Great Deciduous Forest of southern Ohio rife with woodland bison, elk, passenger pigeons, gray wolves, and cougars; or one in the longleaf pine forests, bottomland forests, and canebrakes of the South fat with native wildlife. Or a Tallgrass Prairie National Park of two-million acres in the eastern Great Plains of six-foot-high grass flowing with herds of bison, pronghorn, and elk followed by grizzlies and wolf packs—an American Serengeti. Today, these would be as stunning with their mighty trees, swarming wildlife, and wildness as the great National Parks of the West and even Alaska.

Recognizing their loss, Easterners began to work on what opportunities remained. As early as the 1890s, folks in North Carolina, Tennessee, and Virginia began campaigning for what became Great Smoky Mountains and Shenandoah National Parks. Lands for these National Parks had to be bought from timber companies, farmers, and others. But what of National Forests? Other than northern Minnesota (Superior NF) there were no public lands to withdraw. So, after citizen campaigning, the 1911 Weeks Act authorized the purchase of private lands for National Forests in the East. Today, the National Forests, Parks, and other Federal Public Lands in the East exist because citizens worked hard to get their members of Congress to turn private land into Federal Public Land—and in most cases, it was citizen groups that raised private money to buy the Parks, Forests, and Wildlife Refuges. School kids in Texas saved their lunch money for the fund to buy private ranches to make Big Bend National Park. In other cases, wealthy folks bought land and donated it to the federal government. Sometimes the states did it. More recently, the Land and Water Conservation Fund has provided money.

Another path in the East has been for hikers, campers, hunters, anglers, and other citizens to push their state governments to buy land for state parks, forests, wildlife areas, hunting areas, and so on. States such as New York, Pennsylvania, Michigan, and Wisconsin have done outstanding work in putting together millions of acres of state land (not State School Trust Land) open for public bliss, relaxation, and adventure. Much of this state land came from private land abandoned or foreclosed for nonpayment of taxes in the Great Depression and other hard times.

Do not let the slick lobbyists and legislative hucksters working for the energy, livestock, mining, timber, and development industries hornswoggle you out of your National Parks, National Forests, and other Federal Public Lands. It doesn't matter where you live—Scranton, Pennsylvania, Waycross, Georgia, the Bronx, or East Jesus, Iowa. Yellowstone and Grand Canyon National Parks belong to you. The 400-mile-long Noatak National Wild River in the Brooks Range of Alaska belongs to you. Bosque del Apache National Wildlife Refuge in New Mexico, with tens of thousands of Sandhill Cranes, Snow Geese, and many kinds of ducks flying in at sunset to their night pond, belongs to you. The Mt. Baker-Snoqualmie National Forest in Washington with its soaring 250-foot tall Douglas-firs belongs to you. As do millions of acres of eye-stretching, big-sky land "where the deer and the antelope play."

Since I was born 71 years ago, the slick-tongued bully-boys for the corporate land-raiders have tried to grab OUR Federal Public Lands three times. We've beaten them back each time and we still have our Federal Public Lands. This is the fourth time the land-grabbers have made a play. They are stronger now than ever since they've taken over the Republican Party. The only ones who can stand up to them for our purple mountain majesties and other lands of freedom are we American land patriots. It's your time now. Will you make a stand?

STOP THE LAND GRAB NOW. AGAIN.

Around the Campfire is Dave Foreman's occasional, stirring editorial, which we ran quarterly long ago in Wild Earth magazine, and now run whenever he feels motivated to share a campfire-style story in Rewilding Earth. Previous Around the Campfire editorials (and other articles in this anthology) can be found at rewilding.org.

1   Bernard DeVoto, "The West Against Itself," *Harper's Magazine,* January 1947. DeVoto coined the term "land grab" for the campaign by the cowtown politicians and vested interests in the West to give the Federal Public Lands to the states.

2   Fifth-generation New Mexican, eighth generation west of the Missouri River.

3. There are two exceptions: First, for state sections willingly exchanged for federal lands of equal value; and second, in a few cases, when Eastern states willingly helped to purchase private lands which they then transferred to the National Park Service for new National Parks or to the Forest Service for new National Forests or to the Fish & Wildlife Service for new National Wildlife Refuges.

4. See Dave Foreman, The Great Conservation Divide (Raven's Eye Press, Durango, CO, 2014) for the history of the disposal of the Public Domain and then the withdrawal from disposal of some of the remaining Public Domain for National Parks, Forests, and other systems. For the sake of clarity, I call the lands acquired by the Federal government (those in Table 1) the Public Domain until the early 1890s when the first Forest Reserves were withdrawn along with new National Parks (Yosemite, etc.) at which time I call these withdrawn lands still under the General Land Office (GLO) the Federal Public Lands which were withdrawn from disposal and would remain federal lands whereas the Public Domain was still available for disposal.

5   Foreman, The Great Conservation Divide, 37-50.

6   Dave Foreman, "Comparing Apples and ... Parsnips I," *Around the Campfire #73, The Rewilding Institute, Taos, July 24, 2017.*

7   William K. Wyant, *Westward In Eden: The Public Lands and the Conservation Movement* (University of California Press, Berkeley, 1982), 27. Overall, this is an outstanding and informative book; Chapter 1 "The Public Lands," pages 9-30, is a topnotch rundown of the acquisition and disposal of the Public Domain.

8   Foreman, *Great Conservation Divide, 39-40, explains how this was a necessary compromise to get all thirteen former colonies on board for the Confederation.*

9   That is, except for millions of acres given to the states, granted to railroads, big ranchers, timber companies, and the like often under shady or blatantly corrupt deals. See Foreman, *Great Conservation Divide, 34-50.*

THE ATTACK ON THE NATIONAL PARK SYSTEM

BY JOHN MILES

The National Park System is very popular with the American people: it's nearly overwhelmed with visitors, and it's an American institution we might think the Trump administration would leave alone. We would be wrong.

In its first year the administration has initiated more attacks of potentially devastating consequences for the Park System than any administration since Ronald Reagan, and perhaps since the first national park, Yellowstone, was established in 1872. Parks and other protected areas, like those in the National Wilderness Preservation System and national wildlife refuges, are essential to rewilding America, serving as core habitats for wide-ranging and migrating species in fragmented landscapes. If connectivity for wildlife populations is to be achieved across landscapes, particularly in the American West, national parks must become more, not less, secure in the public land system.

Many actions that threaten the national parks have been proposed in the first year of the Trump administration.[1] Energy production has been prioritized over park protection, the Antiquities Act is being challenged and national monuments downsized, and the President's budget reduces the NPS budget and staffing as visitation grows. At this writing many of the proposed actions are being resisted with litigation, protest (as in public demonstrations and the Outdoor Industry Association moving its shows from Utah), and media coverage of the negative consequences to the parks and other public lands from actions and proposed actions. My goal here is to review what I see as two overarching threats to the National Park System posed by the Trump administration.

The two overarching threats are related. One is a rejection of science as the foundation of policy by the administration, and the second is denial of climate change.[2] Rejection of science as guidance for national park policy did not begin with the Trump administration. Throughout the history of the national parks there has been tension over the purpose of the parks and the mission of the National Park Service. The National Park Act of 1916, establishing the National Park Service, set the stage for this tension when it stated, "the purpose [of parks, monuments, and reservations] is to conserve the scenery and the natural and historic objects and the wild life therein and to provide for the enjoyment of the same in such manner and by such means as will leave them unimpaired for the enjoyment of future generations." [3]

The Park Service was charged with protecting park resources, which would involve science, while providing for "enjoyment," which did not. This set up the tension between conservation and recreation.

Science did not significantly influence national park policy in the early years of the Park Service and has sporadically and often controversially done so since the 1930s when George Melendez Wright launched an initiative to make it integral to park management.[4] In his history of the role of science in preserving nature in national parks, Richard Sellars observed that "ecological preservation and recreational tourism do not have to be mutually exclusive. But in the ebb and flow of national park history, loyalty to traditional assumptions has prevented the Service from establishing unquestioned credentials as a leader in scientifically based land management."[5] Jon Jarvis, NPS Director during the Obama administration, sought to bring science more to the forefront of park management than had recently been the case. He considered climate change an existential threat to the

Courthouse Towers in Arches National Park. © *John Miles*

National Park System in a multitude of ways. To address this, late in his administration, he issued "Director's Order #100: Resource Stewardship for the 21st Century." Its purpose was stated as follows:

"The National Park System and related areas face environmental and social changes that are increasingly widespread, complex, accelerating, and uncertain. Addressing these challenges requires updates of National Park Service (NPS) policy to reflect the complexity of decisions needed for resource stewardship. This Director's Order (Order) is intended to guide the Service in taking the necessary actions to support resource stewardship to fulfill its mission in the 21st century."[6]

On August 16, 2017, Acting NPS Director Michael Reynolds rescinded this order, reportedly at the direction of higher-ranking officials within the Interior Department. The Trump administration's rejection of science and denial of climate change were undoubtedly factors behind this action, though no reason was given by Acting Director Reynolds.

Director Jarvis tasked the National Parks Advisory Board, through its Science Committee, with review of the report issued in 1963 known as the *Leopold Report* (officially *Wildlife Management in the National Parks*). This report had significantly influenced philosophy, policy, and practice of the NPS for fifty years, but the world had changed, and its recommendations were not sufficient to meet the stewardship challenges of the 21st century. Jarvis asked the Committee to consider three questions: "What should be the goals of resource management in the National Park System? What policies for resource management are necessary to achieve these goals? What actions are required to implement these policies?"[7] The Committee submitted its report in August 2012.

The answer to the first question was "to steward NPS resources for continuous change that is not yet fully understood, in order to preserve ecological integrity and cultural and historical authenticity, provide visitors with transformative experiences, and form the core of a national conservation land and seascape."[8] The Service might address these goals by, among other measures, prioritizing "the protection of habitats that may serve as climate refugia, ensuring the maintenance of critical migration and dispersal corridors, and strengthening the resilience of park ecosystems." It should embrace the precautionary principle as the operating guide for its stewardship actions. In answer to the second question, policy and decision making should be based on *"best available sound science, accurate fidelity to the law, and long-term public interest"* (italics in the report)."[9] As to actions required to implement these policies, the Committee emphasized expanding "scientific capacity" of the NPS that might include increased monitoring, citizen science, and especially increased training in science for managers, including park superintendents.

When Jarvis issued Director's Order #100 four years later, it reflected all of the recommendations of the Science Committee, using much of the language in the *Revisiting Leopold* report. In its "Background" section it states:

"Climate change is creating and will continue to drive dynamic environmental shifts that affect natural and cultural resources, facilities, visitation patterns, and visitor experiences. Additional pressures such as biodiversity loss, invasive species, land use changes, and pollution are accelerating. New Scientific information and new disciplines of science have expanded our understanding of natural and cultural systems, and revealed that much is still unknown about how these systems function."[10]

It emphasized integrating natural and cultural resource stewardship and stated that "This integration recognizes the impact of humans on their environment and the impact of a changing environment on humans."[11] These passages alone may have been the trigger for rescission of the Order with their mention of climate change and emphasis on science.

On January 15, 2017, nine of the twelve members of the National Parks Advisory Board resigned citing frustration that they were being ignored. The Director's Order, in part a product of their work, was rescinded without any consultation with them, and when the Board chair, Tony Knowles, requested a meeting with the new administration, there was no answer. Asked why the members resigned, Knowles said, "By nine of us resigning, we felt we'd be able to get the microphone briefly to at least talk to the American people about climate change, about preserving the natural diversity of wildlife, about making sure underrepresented minorities not only come to the parks but are employees there."[12] No public process was involved in revoking the Director's Order, and Knowles said, "We had strongly supported it, but these things were just done, so these were the disappointments we had."[13]

All of this adds up to turmoil about "America's Best Idea" as filmmaker Ken Burns titled his series on America's national parks. There is no Advisory Board, no NPS Director, and clear signals that the Trump Administration wishes to take the National Park System in new directions that do not recognize climate change and do not emphasize the primacy of science in stewardship of park resources.

Trump Attacks On Our Natural Heritage

President Theodore Roosevelt embarked on his Great Loop tour of the American West in 1903, to that time the longest cross-country journey ever taken by a President of the United States. His purpose was to present his conservation policies in the run-up to the 1904 presidential election. One stop on the tour was the Grand Canyon, dismissively called by locals the "Big Ditch" which was, to developers, a useless waste, like Death Valley. Roosevelt saw it differently, and speaking at the Canyon rim he said the following to his audience of Arizonans:

"I want to ask you to do one thing in connection with it. In your own interest and the interest of all the country keep this great wonder of nature as it now is. I hope you won't have a building of any kind to mar the grandeur and sublimity of the cañon. You cannot improve upon it. The ages have been at work on it, and man can only mar it. Keep it for your children and your children's children and all who come after you as one of the great sights for all Americans to see."[14]

These words, oft-quoted today, are in sharp contrast to the view of public lands of the Trump administration which is intent on "improving" all public lands by development of one sort or another. Trump disagrees with Roosevelt's view that some places are of "such interest of all the country" that they should be preserved.

Roosevelt spoke these words before there was an Antiquities Act, a National Park Service, and a Grand Canyon National Monument and then Park. Under the Trump administration, we see three basic threats to the National Park System: the drive to change or kill the Antiquities Act; the effort to prioritize recreation at the expense of other park values; and the trend of development around and even within units of the National Park System and other protected areas.

The Antiquities Act has been the object of anger since its passage in 1906 because it preserved parts of the public domain, stopping destruction by those who would exploit those places. Iowa congressman John Lacey, concerned especially about the plundering of artifacts from Mesa Verde and other Southwest archaeological sites and of Pliocene fossils, pottery shards, and petrified logs from the Painted Desert-Petrified Forest area, pushed through Congress the Act, which he had drafted with archaeologist Edgar Hewett. President Roosevelt, of course, was all for legislation that would allow him to take "rapid presidential action" in the face of a "tortoise-paced Congress."[15] He did just that, creating eighteen national monuments, including Grand Canyon where miners were intent on digging for various minerals. Congressman Lacey inserted the words "scenic and scientific" into the Antiquities Act in order that it could be used to protect places like Petrified Forest. Roosevelt interpreted it as a means to protect the vastness of the Grand Canyon.

Thanks to Lacey and Roosevelt, the Antiquities Act has been an effective tool for conservation. Most early monuments became part of the National Park System, carved out of public land sometimes managed by the Forest Service or other agencies and placed in the care of the Park Service. Recently monument proclamations have left them to be managed by the agency managing the land in question, as with the Bureau of Land Management in the case of Grand Staircase-Escalante and Bears Ears. In 2018 President Trump is attempting to reverse monument proclamations by executive order, and anti-conservation congressmen, principally from Utah, are proposing outright revocation or at least revision of the Antiquities Act. Weakening or revoking this conservation tool, which allows a President to take executive action to protect places "of interest of all the country" in the face of threat and congressional inaction, would be a huge loss since there are many excellent candidates for national monument status still awaiting action.

The second threat involves the tightrope the Park Service has walked since 1916 when the National Park Service Act charged it with providing for the "enjoyment of the same in such manner and by such means as will leave them unimpaired for the enjoyment of future generations." The "same" here are "national parks, monuments, and reservations."[16] The balance has swung back and forth between making the parks accessible for recreation and preserving park resources, with tension always present between the two missions. The National Park System has grown dramatically since 1916, and so of course has American and global population. Park visitation has grown from tens of thousands to more than 300 million a year. Outdoor recreation has grown in popularity, and types of recreational activity have multiplied. The growth in demand for national park experiences has vastly outpaced the growth of the National Park System.

The challenge for rewilding is to promote strategies of managing recreation that result in the least impact on the natural world in national parks and other protected areas. There are short-term and long-term aspects of this challenge. Urgent issues in 2018 include Department of the Interior rescission of NPS Director's Order #100 that emphasized, on the nature side of park management, use of science and goals of connectivity and life-cycle stewardship. This Trump administration action was applauded by the Access Fund, the Outdoor Recreation Roundtable, and the American Recreation Coalition, signaling their concern that stewardship aimed at conservation will constrain opportunity for recreation, which often involves development. Interior Secretary Ryan Zinke, an avid hunter, established a "Hunting and Shooting Sports Conservation Council" the purpose of which, a press release indicated, is to advise the Interior and Agriculture Departments on "policies and authorities with regard to wildlife and habitat conservation." The National Park System is the last public land system to constrain hunting within its domain—essentially all other federal public lands are open to hunting and trapping—and rumors abound as to what the implications of Zinke's actions might mean for the System. These are only two examples of pressing issues in 2018.

Over the longer term, the challenge is to develop and promote policies that facilitate outdoor recreation while conserving wildlife and other sensitive natural resources. Policy and stewardship in national parks (and elsewhere in the outdoor recreation world) must be guided by research and knowledge, not by the economics of the outdoor recreation industry, which should work with managers to find balance. Some places can handle motorized access while others cannot. Some are appropriate for bolted climbs, mountain bikes, and paragliders; others are not. Constraints on activity to protect natural and cultural values can and must be agreed to by all, and that will not be easy, but if values of parks are to be protected for the interest of all the country, world, and future generations, that must be the goal.

The third and last threat is development, both outside and inside national parks, and there are short and long-term challenges here as well. Short-term examples from the first year of the Trump administration are: review and revise oil and gas leasing in marine environments (Executive Order 13795); review and revise regulations that hamper energy development on public lands (DOI Secretarial Order 3349); move to approve groundwater mining of 16 billion gallons per year from the Mojave Desert; BLM approval of a pumped storage facility near Joshua Tree National Park; push a road through part of Gates of the Arctic National Park and Preserve to allow mining near Ambler, Alaska; sell oil and gas leases near Chaco Culture National Historic Park—the list could go on and on. The response to these immediate threats is straightforward—oppose the actions one by one with every tool available.

The challenge is different over the long term. In a world bent on eternal economic growth, the underlying premise is that humans have infinite needs and nature has an infinite capacity to meet those needs. But the earth is finite. Parks and protected areas in a world driven by this premise will be islands in a rising sea of development. Ultimately, they will be overwhelmed. In the medium term, pumpjacks and fracking towers will be everywhere, corridors for wildlife blocked in a multitude of ways. Global population growth will bring more demand for shrinking parks and protected areas, which will be "loved to death." As greater portions of this population have less and less contact with nature, "ecological amnesia" will be rampant—if you haven't experienced it, you won't miss it. Support for parks and protected areas will decline, as will opposition to develop around and even in them.

Call To Action

This is not a pretty picture, but it cannot be ignored. America was the birthplace of the national park idea and led the way in protecting places of "interest of all the country" and, we should add, the world. America can lead again in conserving natural and cultural legacies. At this time such a prospect seems far from certain, but there are ways we can help. Keep up on immediate threats to individual park units, as with the current reductions of Bears Ears and Grand Staircase-Escalante National Monuments (even though they are BLM monuments—they are all part of the public land monument system). The best places to keep current on park issues are NPCA.org and Nationalparkstraveler.org. Study your favorite parks and their issues, and share your expertise with Congress, the Department of Interior (even if the fox is guarding this henhouse at the moment), or whomever you think needs to hear from you. Let Congress, the NPS, and other decision-makers know you think science must be the foundation of park and protected area stewardship. Be part of the growing activist movement to protect the national parks and all public lands.

1   For actions taken during the first year of the Trump administration, see Policy Update, Dec. 4, 2017, "The Undoing of Our Public Lands and National Parks" at *www.npca.org/articles.*

2   A comprehensive look at both of these issues is Shawn Otto, *The War on Science: Who's Waging It, Why it Matters, What We Can Do About It.* (Minneapolis, MN.: Milkweed Editions, 2016.)

3   An Act to Establish a National Park Service, and for Other Purposes, Approved August 25, 1916 (39 Stat. 535).

4   See Richard West Sellars, *Preserving Nature in the National Parks: A History.* (New Haven: Yale University Press, 1997).

5   Sellars, *Preserving Nature in National Parks,* p. 284.

6   Director's Order #100: p. 1.

7   Cover letter to Jonathan Jarvis from Tony Knowles and Rita Colwell, for *Revisiting Leopold: Resource Stewardship in the National Parks, A Report of the National Parks Advisory Board Science Committee, August 25, 2012.*

8   *Revisiting Leopold,* p. 11.

9   *Revisiting Leopold,* p. 17.

10 Director's Order #100, p. 2

11 Director's Order #100, p. 4.

12 Krista Langlois, "Why the National Park Advisory Board Imploded," *High Country News,* Jan. 18, 2018.

13 Quoted by Rob Hotakainen, "Zinke's 'crazy policies' Sparked Resignations," *Greenwire,* January 17, 2018.

14 Quoted in Douglas Brinkley, *Wilderness Warrior: Theodore Roosevelt and the Crusade for America.* (New York: Harper, 2009), p.527.

15 Robert W. Righter, "National Monuments to National Parks: The Use of the Antiquities Act of 1906," *Western Historical Quarterly*, Vol. 20, No. 3 (August 1989), pp. 281-301, cited in Brinkley, p. 643.

16 An Act to Establish a National Park Service, and for Other Purposes, Approved August 25, 1916 (39 Stat. 535).

FOREST PROTECTION IN THE TRUMP ERA

BY DOUGLAS BEVINGTON

In the wake of the 2016 election, the arrival of the Trump administration and the new Congress has been bad news for our national forests. Members of the new administration and Congress are pushing to more than double the amount of logging on our national forests. However, by directly confronting the misinformation they use to attack public land protection, the environmental community has an important opportunity to overcome some recent constraints and revitalize broad support for genuine forest protection.

The dangers from the new administration and Congress were recently demonstrated by a legislative rider on the omnibus budget bill passed in March 2018 that created a large new categorical exclusion for logging on national forests. Categorical exclusions are used by the Forest Service to circumvent environmental review and public oversight. In theory, categorical exclusions are intended for projects that are so obviously benign that they do not need regular environmental review, but in practice, the Forest Service is trying to use them as cover for harmful logging projects. For example, the Center for Biological Diversity and John Muir Project are currently litigating a categorical exclusion for the "Sunny South" logging project that seeks to cut in six of the best remaining spotted owl territories in California's Sierra Nevada.

The new categorical exclusion enacted by Congress and the Trump administration allows for large logging projects up to 3,000 acres in size each. To put this number in perspective,

3,000 acres is nearly four times the size of Central Park in New York. Furthermore, because the rider contains no restrictions to prevent multiple projects from being put next to each other, the overall affected area could be huge.

So how did this dangerous rider become law? Logging proponents relied on misleading claims about forest fire to justify the CE. While many environmental groups opposed the rider, some organizations provided tacit or explicit support for it because they have embraced erroneous claims about fire and logging. A remarkable divergence has emerged over the past fifteen years between the state of the science on large forest fires and the positions taken by some environmental organizations on issues related to fire. The Trump administration is now taking advantage of this divide.

In the early 2000s, most environmental groups were openly critical of George W. Bush's so-called Healthy Forest Initiative, calling it "Orwellian" to depict efforts to increase logging on national forests as "protecting" those forests from fire. However, at that point, the science on the ecological role of mixed-severity forest fire was far less developed, so it was easier for logging proponents to portray big forest fires as "catastrophic" and more logging (rebranded as "thinning") as the solution. In this setting, environmental groups that challenged logging were often blamed for the wildfires that inevitably occurred, and they did not have that many scientific resources to respond to those criticisms.

Faced with this criticism, some organizations decided to join "collaborative" processes with the Forest Service and timber industry that promoted logging under the rubric of fire reduction. This trend increased during the Obama years. By the time the Trump administration arrived, many of the groups involved in collaboratives had reduced their independent scientific and legal capacity to challenge harmful logging projects that used fire as a justification.

Post-fire logging after the massive 2013 Rim Fire in the Stanislaus National Forest in California. © Doug Bevington

Environmental groups that mainly reference Forest Service claims about fire wound up taking positions that were closely aligned with the agency. They endorsed large-scale logging projects done under the banner of fire reduction. They advocated for more funding for the Forest Service to subsidize those projects. Some of those organizations even intervened on behalf of the Forest Service against lawsuits by other environmental groups challenging the harms from those projects. And some organizations supported legislation that reduced public oversight and legal review of fire-related logging projects. Recently, the Trump administration and new Congress were able to use some of those organizations to help get the new categorical exclusion legislation passed.

Ironically, over the past fifteen years, the scientific research on large wildfires grew rapidly in a very different direction. While logging proponents vilified intense fires as being "catastrophic" and portraying them as an aberration, scientists produced a growing body of research showing that large, intense mixed-severity fires are a natural and ecologically important component of most forest ecosystems in the western United States. New research techniques for analyzing historical fire patterns showed that there had been significantly more fire in the past, including more high-severity fire, compared to current levels. And it was discovered that the patches of high-severity within mixed-severity forest fires created a unique habitat—"complex early seral forest," also called "snag forest"—that has some of the highest levels of wildlife diversity and abundance of any forest type.

However, the Forest Service kept promoting the idea that fire was a problem that needed to be reduced through more logging, with most timber sales on national forest now being done under various fire-related justifications. Likewise, some Forest Service-affiliated scientists produced studies that gave cover for those fire-related logging claims, but their studies were marred by significant omissions and errors.

For example, the Forest Service frequently claims that if fire is simply allowed to return to "overstocked" areas where it was previously suppressed, those forests will now burn at mostly high severity. The Forest Service uses that claim to contend that logging is necessary as a precondition to restoring fire. However, when independent scientists tested this question empirically by examining fire severity patterns in three major fires, they found that previously suppressed areas burned mostly at low and moderate severity.

In response, Forest Service scientists published a paper claiming to have shown the suppressed areas burned hotter. However, when the independent scientists looked at the methodology of the response paper, they found that its authors had cherry-picked the data. The response paper included only one of the three fires from the original study and it conflated two analytical categories in order to get results that matched the agency's claims. In contrast, when all of the available data were used with the proper analytical categories, the independent scientists showed that forests where fire had long been suppressed did not burn at significantly higher severity. And at this point, there are at least four other empirical studies that support the independent scientists' findings about fire behavior in forests where fire had been suppressed. In other words, the Forest Service's main fire-related justification for logging is based on erroneous claims.

The results of independent research on fire ecology have big policy implications for our national forests. While the Forest Service calls for more and more funding to subsidize massive logging projects across vast landscapes under the claim that it is needed to protect forests for fire, the latest fire science shows that this logging is unnecessary and even harmful to the many forest plants and animals that benefit from the habitat created by mixed-severity fire.

Massive logging projects are also unnecessary from a human-safety perspective. Whether a house burns during a wildfire is largely determined by the conditions within 100-200 feet of the house and the house itself (roof materials, vent screens, etc.), not by logging projects off in remote wildlands. From a fiscal and practical perspective, work on the space immediately around houses is far less costly and more readily achievable than large-scale logging projects. Yet, the Forest Service's continued emphasis on expensive subsidized logging projects pulls resources and attention away from needed work around homes.

The latest science shows the opportunity for a new approach to fire management on our national forests. Mixed-severity fire is a natural and beneficial component of western forest ecosystems. Our national forests need more mixed-severity fire, including the high-severity fire component. And the good news is that we can allow mixed-severity fire to return to our national forests without landscape-wide logging as a prerequisite. And some of the resources that have been used to subsidize logging on national forests could instead be redirected to bolster work right around houses so that communities adjacent to forests can safely coexist with the inevitable fires.

In contrast, the logging-based approach currently promoted by the Forest Service and its allies is expensive, complicated, and damaging to forests, while diverting resources from substantive home safety actions. It has also led to repeated efforts to weaken environmental laws in order to increase logging, including the new Trump-era categorical exclusion.

It is troubling that some environmental organizations are still providing support for the Forest Service approach and missing out on the exciting policy implications of the latest science. What can explain this?

In part, it may simply reflect organizational inertia. If a group has been involved for years in promoting logging projects with the Forest Service as a "win-win" solution, it can be difficult to admit that the science now shows that those projects were unnecessary and even harmful. Also, participants in collaborative processes have often come to rely heavily on the Forest Service for their information about fire science, and this filter has meant that they are not aware of many of the recent developments in the science or have been encouraged to discount studies that refute the Forest Service's claims.

The arrival of the Trump administration is a wake-up call that our national forests are not safe from logging proponents who will readily use any pretext to dramatically increase cutting. It is time for the environmental community to take a deep look at the latest fire science, consider its policy implications, and make a choice—are we going to provide cover for the latest excuses to take more trees out of our national forests, or are we going take action to prevent harmful logging projects?

Unless we bridge the current gap between the latest science on the ecological importance of mixed-severity fire and the outdated positions of some environmental groups regarding "catastrophic" fire, the Trump administration and new Congress are all too ready to exploit this gap to do tremendous harm to our national forests. On the other hand, if we embrace this science, we have a great opportunity to take the lead in supporting genuine forest protection policies that are better ecologically and economically, and are more effective in helping communities safely coexist with fire-dependent forests.

What You Can Do:

1. Learn about the ecological value of mixed-severity forest fires to help refute erroneous fire-related pretexts for logging. Some good collections of the latest scientific studies have been compiled by the Wild Nature Institute (wildnatureinstitute.org) and John Muir Project (johnmuirproject.org), as well as in *The Ecological Importance of Mixed-Severity Fires: Nature's Phoenix,* by Dominick DellaSalla and Chad Hanson.

2. Support the grassroots forest protection groups that are most vigorously challenging new logging projects on our national forests. Some examples of bold groups in various parts of the country can be found among the list of grantees of the Fund for Wild Nature (fundwildnature.org).

3. Contact your elected representatives and urge them to protect our national forests from harmful commercial logging, including projects done under fire-related pretexts. Call the Capitol switchboard at 202-224-3121.

BLM UNDER TRUMP AND ZINKE: A DISASTER FOR PUBLIC LANDS

BY GEORGE WUERTHNER

When I was a kid, I was athletic and one of my favorite games in elementary school was dodge ball. In this game, someone goes to the center of a ring of other kids and attempts to "dodge" a soccer ball thrown at them. You get to stay in the ring until hit by a ball. Then the person who "knocked" the person out of the ring, moves into the center and becomes the new target.

I was quick on my feet and could usually dodge any ball thrown at me. But after many attempts to dislodge me from the center of the circle, the gym teacher would throw out a few more balls. With 3-4 balls all coming at me from different directions, I was unable to duck them all and was soon hit.

I think the same strategy is operating with the Trump Administration under the direction of Secretary of Interior Ryan Zinke. They are playing dodge ball with our national heritage by throwing out so many development proposals that no one can effectively keep up with them, much less thwart them all. Zinke and Trump know that at least some of their administration "balls" will get through to strike their target, which can be characterized as reducing all regulations, enhancing opportunities for private profit and development at public expense, and giving away as much of the public domain and resources as possible.

The agency that is feeling most of these deregulation and giveaway efforts is the federal Bureau of Land Management.

The Bureau of Land Management (BLM) is under the Department of Interior overseen by Secretary of Interior Ryan Zinke. The BLM administers more land in the United States than any other land management agency, with more than 245 million acres under its control. It also is the main agency with jurisdiction over sub-surface mineral estate on 700 million acres of land (i.e. it administers mineral issues under the authority of the Forest Service, Park Service, and Fish & Wildlife Service, and even some private landowners).

Much of the domain under BLM control is the "lands nobody wanted." The agency was created in 1946 from the union of two other federal agencies: the Grazing Service and General Land Office. The past historical missions of these two agencies have influenced the BLM's ongoing management of public lands. Often known derisively as the "Bureau of Livestock and Mining," the BLM has gradually moved to reflect the change in American public values for greater protection of natural areas and wildlife by the establishment of Wilderness Areas, National Monuments, and Areas of Critical Environmental Concern, among other designations.

The Trump administration has focused on dismantling as many of the environmental protections and land designations as possible. One method is the use of "categorical exclusion" or CEs to allow any development to go forward without the need for an Environmental Impact Statement if the BLM can assert that there will be no "major" environmental impacts. (The Forest Service increasingly uses CEs to facilitate logging without environmental review, as Doug Bevington explains in his article, this volume.)

New policies are designed to limit public participation in decision-making about public lands. For instance, new regulations call for limits on the number of pages in any Environmental Impact Statement, as well as limits on the Freedom of Information Act.

In another example of the Trump administration's industry-friendly policies, the BLM has been directed to process oil and gas

Bobbye at Calf Creek, Grand Staircase Escalante National Monument, Utah. © *George Wuerthner*

leases within six months and shorten public challenges to leases to ten days.

In addition, the Trump administration seems driven to dismantle any programs, regulations or environmental protections created under the Obama administration. For example, Ryan Zinke has recommended massive reductions in the size of two Obama and Clinton era national monuments: Bears Ears and Grand Staircase Escalante. Indeed, the Bears Ears boundaries were reduced by 85%; and almost immediately, the Interior Department put much of the area up for oil and gas leasing.

Interior Department documents obtained by Freedom of Information requests show that Interior Secretary Zinke worked extensively with the energy industry to define the boundary reductions at Bears Ears and Grand Staircase Escalante.

In addition to Bears Ears leasing, the BLM plans to permit leasing in a number of other canyon country special areas including the BLM's Canyons of the Ancients National Monument, adjacent Cross Canyon, and proposed wilderness areas in Goldbar Canyon and Labyrinth Canyon near Moab, Utah.

Zinke has also recommended reducing the size of Cascade-Siskiyou National Monument in Oregon to open lands for logging old growth timber.

In a similar manner, Zinke and the Trump administration have opened the coastal plain of Arctic National Wildlife Refuge to potential oil and gas development. Congress and President Trump lifted a 40-year drilling ban on the refuge as the GOP tax bill was approved in December. Oil and gas leasing could begin there in 2019.

The Arctic Coastal Plain is the only portion of the refuge that is not currently designated Wilderness, which would preclude such development. The coastal plain is the most important wildlife area in the entire refuge and home to polar bears, caribou, musk oxen, wolves, Arctic fox and many nesting bird species. For decades, there have been attempts to obtain Wilderness designation as a means of precluding energy development. Ignoring all the past recognition of Arctic Refuge's ecological value, the administration is working to develop the coastal plain, which once dotted with roads, oil wells, and pipelines will no longer qualify for Wilderness designation.

Also in Alaska, the BLM is currently reviewing a proposal to build a 220-mile road from the Pipeline Haul Road (Dalton Highway) to the Ambler Mining District near the headwaters of the Kobuk River. The proposed road would cross several Wild and Scenic Rivers and part of Gates of the Arctic National Park and potentially open up much of the southern Brooks Range to future development.

The Trump Administration is "streamlining" energy development within sage grouse habitat. One of the reasons sage grouse were not listed under the Endangered Species Act was due to new Obama era regulations that were designed to protect the bird's habitat as Priority Habitat Management Areas. But the BLM under Zinke's direction plans to reclassify millions of acres of the bird's habitat to permit more oil and gas development.

The Trump administration has begun to dismantle the new Fracking Rule which was implemented under the Obama administration. The rule was stayed by a court, but it set standards for well construction, wastewater management, and chemical disclosure on public lands. This rule aimed to protect groundwater from chemical pollution caused by fracking operations. It also prohibited drilling in habitat for endangered species like the sage grouse.

And it's not just oil and gas development that has been targeted for expedited leasing. The BLM has also proposed expansion of coal leases on 15 million acres (an area as big as Vermont, New Hampshire, and Connecticut combined) in the Powder River Basin of eastern Montana and Wyoming.

In February 2018, the Trump administration began a review of BLM's Desert Renewable Energy Conservation Plan.

The plan, adopted by the Obama administration, was designed to limit any renewable energy development such as wind, solar, and geothermal to less fragile parts of the California desert. The original plan set aside 6.5 million acres out of 10.8 million acres for conservation. Approximately 800,000 acres were considered suitable for renewable energy development.

Besides his aggressive measures to increase energy development on BLM lands, Secretary Zinke has not forgotten his cozy relationship with the West's public lands ranchers (like Cliven Bundy). In keeping with its original founding as the Grazing Service, the BLM administers grazing privileges for 18,000 livestock producers on 155 million acres of public land. That is more acreage than the entire states of Montana and Idaho combined.

Soon after the election, the Trump administration slashed the existing ridiculously low grazing fee from $1.87 an AUM to $1.41 AUM (AUM= Animal Unit Month or the amount of forage consumed by a cow and calf in a month). AUMs leased on private lands are often $20 or more.

One new Trump initiative is Outcome-Based Grazing Authorizations , which will be implemented on 6-12 areas and will allow greater "flexibility" to ranchers. 'Flexibility' is always code for less supervision and oversight of public lands.

In addition, the administration is supporting legislation in Congress that would open any "vacant" grazing allotments to new grazing leases. Many vacant leases exist in wilderness areas and other sensitive landscapes and could be reopened to livestock production.

Similarly problematic yet barely noticed by mainstream media, the BLM has launched a number of questionable efforts to reduce range fires under the guise of protecting sage grouse. For instance, the BLM is developing a plan for massive "fuel breaks" spread across thousands of acres of the Great Basin, which would fragment habitat and in many cases facilitate the spread of cheatgrass, a flammable exotic that increases fire risk.

In other areas, the BLM has engaged in a giant juniper removal program, across tens of thousands of acres of public land, ostensibly to reduce fires and expand habitat for sage grouse. Ranchers believe juniper reduces grass growth, which is the real reason for juniper removal.

In short, if you are a mining company, oil and gas company, rancher or other commodity producer, you love what the BLM is doing on public lands. The Trump administration's basic aim is to expand the privatization of public resources for private gain.

What You Can Do:

I hate to be partisan, but the obvious thing is to make sure you vote and remove the GOP and Trump hegemony that now controls public lands. If you live in a state with Democratic members of Congress, make sure they know of these and future detrimental proposals and changes in regulation. Beyond that, there are many people working in the BLM who love our public lands, but they need the support of citizens to counter the worst abuses of this administration. Go to public meetings. Ask questions. Get involved. Stand up for the many federal employees who favor protecting our public lands.

POPULATION

Petroglyph-style Hand. © *Karen Borger*

WHY FAMILY PLANNING IS GOOD FOR PEOPLE AND THE PLANET

BY SUZANNE YORK, TRANSITION EARTH

Given the state of the world today, it is urgent that humanity and nature exist in balance. The burden, of course, is on people to make this happen. In a world of 7.7 billion people that could grow to 10 billion by 2050, we are making this more difficult.

It doesn't have to be that way. We know what must be done, but we must find the political and societal/cultural will to make it happen, in a manner that supports having a proper conversation about best approaches. The solutions to attaining a healthy population number are grounded in the principles of rights and empowerment, and they are things the world should be doing anyway.

Support Family Planning Globally And Locally

One of the first things to do is invest in women's health, particularly by providing voluntary family planning services. This is often considered "low-hanging fruit," as it is the right thing to do, relatively easy to provide, and something most women want. Everyone should have the right to plan if and when to have a family, and have the tools, resources and access to do so, or not do so.

There are 214 million women in developing regions who want to delay or avoid pregnancy but are not using a modern contraceptive method.[1] Of the estimated 206 million pregnancies in 2017 in developing regions, 43 percent were unintended (they occurred too soon or were not wanted at all).

The estimated current annual cost of providing modern contraceptive services in developing regions is $6.3 billion, including direct and indirect costs.[2] If this were to be expanded and improved to address all women's needs for modern contraception (in developing regions), it would amount to $12.1 billion annually.

Just to put that in perspective, Americans spent $9 billion last year celebrating Halloween[3] and $56 billion to attend sporting events.[4] The budget for the U.S. Defense Department is more than $700 billion.

The good news is that we know what to do, how to do it, and why to do it. Let's look at just two examples of why investing in family planning can make a huge difference in people's lives: Uganda and the United States.

Most of Sub-Saharan Africa is experiencing the highest rates of population growth in the world. In fact, all of Africa's population is expected to double, from 1 billion today to 2.6 billion by 2050.[5]

One of the continent's fastest growing countries is Uganda. Its current population of 42 million is projected to reach 100 million by 2050 and it is one of the world's youngest countries, with more than 75% of the population under the age of 30. It is equivalent in geographic size to the state of Oregon, which has a population of 5 million people.

One in four girls between the ages of 15 to 19 in Uganda[6] has given birth or is carrying her first child, according to the country's 2016 Demographic and Health Survey.[7] Reducing teen pregnancies will result in greater education and economic opportunities for youth. Meeting the reproductive rights and needs of youth through education, outreach and access to services is imperative. Local organizations such as Reproductive Health

*Central to addressing the human overpopulation crisis
is rewarding small, close families.*
© Steven Kellogg

107

Uganda (rhu.or.ug) are working with youth to raise awareness and access to contraceptives and family planning services.

In the United States, 45% of pregnancies are unplanned. The state of Colorado worked to change this situation through the Colorado Family Planning Initiative which provided training, support and low- or no-cost long-acting reversible contraceptives (LARCs) to low-income women, especially teens.[8]

Colorado made more progress than any other state in reducing unplanned pregnancies. The Department of Public Health & Environment reported that teen pregnancies were nearly cut in half and that the initiative "empowered thousands of Colorado women to choose when and whether to start a family."[9] Colorado's experience is a model for other states.

Climate, Carbon, And Family Planning

What happens when climate impacts become more severe? Given the alarming predictions on our warming planet, family planning offers an overlooked path forward to better cope with climate change.

A recent report by Population Reference Bureau on family planning and climate change adaptation notes that "Regions of high population growth, high fertility, and high unmet need for family planning frequently overlap with regions of high vulnerability to climate change."[10]

An increasing body of evidence points to the links between women's met needs for family planning with reduced human vulnerability to climate change and improved resilience in the face of climate change impacts.

The continued unmet need for family planning by women in regions of rapid population growth can exacerbate vulnerability and limit the adaptive capacity of individuals, households, and communities. The above referenced PRB report states that meeting women's needs for family planning in these regions has multiple important benefits, including:

- Women and their children are healthier—an essential building block of resilience;
- Smaller families result in reduced household demand on climate-sensitive resources like food and water, and can result in increased time for women's engagement in climate adaptation-related activities.
- Population stabilization reduces both pressure on local natural resources and the sheer scale of human vulnerability to climate change impacts.

Increasingly, climate researchers and activists see the connection. In Drawdown: The Most Comprehensive Plan Ever Proposed to Reverse Global Warming, researchers saw the link between women's rights and climate change. Among the report's main solutions is a combination of educating girls and supporting family planning, which together could reduce emissions by 120 gigatons of CO_2 equivalent by 2050—more than on- and offshore wind power combined (99 GT).

A growing number of organizations are calling for population and family planning to be included in climate adaptation proposals and projects.

Biodiversity Protection And Family Planning

Some of the places of greatest biodiversity on the planet are experiencing rapid population growth, habitat loss, and development. Forests in particular play a critical part in climate stabilization, and are under grave threat. A recent report by World Wildlife Fund found that the world's forests and areas of great biodiversity could lose more than half of their plant species by the end of the century unless countries seriously work to reduce the effects of climate change.[11]

According to Rainforest Action Network, Indonesia has one of the highest deforestation rates in the world, and even conservative studies suggest that over a million hectares (2.4 million acres) of Indonesian rainforest is cleared annually.[12] Although the Indonesian government has invested in education and awareness of contraception, thereby lowering the total fertility rate, the current population of 261 million is still increasing and by 2050 it is projected to be the world's seventh largest country.

Biodiversity loss is happening in affluent countries too. Australia, for example—where nearly 85% of the country's plants, 84% of its mammals, and 45% of its birds are found nowhere else—is losing forests at an alarming rate.

Australia has the unfortunate distinction of being the only developed country to be included on World Wildlife Fund's global deforestation front, as the country is projected to lose 3 million hectares of forest in the next 15 years.[13] In southwest Australia, 89% of amphibians could become extinct.

As for the United States, the Trump administration is rolling back environmental protections almost as fast as it is gutting reproductive rights domestically and family planning assistance internationally. This is detrimental to nature and humans.

Today, there are more than 1.5 billion people living in the world's biodiversity hotspots—areas of highly-endangered flora and fauna found nowhere else on the planet that lack government protection and are under intense human pressure. As climate change affects more and more communities around the world, it becomes urgent to incorporate a holistic approach to mitigating and adapting to the increasingly severe and unpredictable conditions.

This calls for new thinking about conservation, climate change, and communities. One effective approach is the development model known as Population, Health, and Environment, or PHE. This is an integrated solution linking family planning, public health, and conservation that recognizes the interconnectedness of people and their local environment. It is an acknowledgement of the direct links between the reproductive health of individuals (both men and women); the health of communities living in remote biodiversity-rich areas; and the health of the natural environment, or ecosystem, upon which all life depends. PHE can greatly strengthen community resilience to environmental problems.

It's All Connected

Support for a healthy and thriving population requires a multi-pronged approach, because it is all connected. Overconsumption and unsustainable resource use is a huge problem that must also be tackled. Humanity is living beyond the carrying capacity of Earth. Poverty and inequity—main drivers of population growth—need to be eliminated. Women should have land rights. Men need to be involved in family planning. We must reform the economic system, which is unsustainably based on perpetual growth. And to really move the needle on saving the planet calls for new approaches, such as recognizing rights of nature.

Which takes us back to the beginning of this article and the imperative to live in balance with nature. We need to act smarter about the way we do things, and we need to start today. We need to undertake many difficult endeavors—let's start with something easier and support reproductive rights and family planning. It will benefit both people and the planet for a long time to come.

How To Help

Call on your elected representatives to stop cuts to international family planning assistance.

Become informed about and support policies and legislation that empower women—health, gender equality, and reproductive rights (reducing unintended pregnancies, greater access to birth control).

Call on your congressional representative to co-sponsor the *Global Health, Empowerment, and Rights Act* ("the Global HER Act"), which calls for repealing the Global Gag Rule that threatens U.S. funding of global organizations working on family planning and reproductive health.[14]

Call on your congressional representative to co-sponsor the *Women and Climate Change Act of 2018* to develop coordinated strategies to mitigate the impact of climate change on women and girls around the world.[15]

Protest cuts to reproductive health and access to contraceptives in the U.S., and back organizations fighting for women's rights.

Protest cuts to environmental protections and climate change initiatives in the U.S., and back organizations fighting for nature.

Involve men in voluntary family planning programs.

Vote!

---

1. https://www.unfpa.org/family-planning
2. https://www.guttmacher.org/fact-sheet/adding-it-up-contraception-mnh-2017
3. https://www.forbes.com/sites/sleasca/2017/10/30/halloween-spending-halloween-candy/#507c103d20a1
4. https://www.cnbc.com/2017/09/11/americans-spend-56-billion-on-sporting-events.html
5. https://www.prb.org/2017-world-population-data-sheet/
6. http://www.pathfinder.org/countries/uganda/
7. http://www.ubos.org/onlinefiles/uploads/ubos/pdf%252
8. https://www.colorado.gov/pacific/cdphe/cfpi-report
9. https://www.colorado.gov/pacific/cdphe/cfpi-report
10. http://www.prb.org/Publications/Articles/2018/Building-Resilience-Through-Family-Planning-and-Adaptation-Finance.aspx
11. https://www.worldwildlife.org/press-releases/half-of-plant-and-animal-species-at-risk-from-climate-change-in-world-s-most-important-natural-places
12. https://www.ran.org/indonesian-rainforests
13. https://www.theguardian.com/environment/2018/mar/05/global-deforestation-hotspot-3m-hectares-of-australian-forest-to-be-lost-in-15-years
14. http://www.genderhealth.org/files/uploads/change/publications/CHANGE_Global_HER_Act_fact_sheet.pdf
15. http://wedo.org/u-s-women-climate-change-act-2018/

DARING TO TELL THE TRUTH ABOUT SUSTAINABILITY

BY TERRY SPAHR, *8 BILLION ANGELS* EXECUTIVE PRODUCER AND EARTH OVERSHOOT FOUNDER

In my short lifetime I have observed human economic activities and interactions that negatively impact our world with greater frequency and with greater severity.

I desired to better understand these signs, their frequencies, trends, patterns and causes; to separate fact from fiction; and to determine what these activities, individually or as a whole, mean for my future, my children's future, and the future all of the world's inhabitants.

Due to human ingenuity and the discovery and commercialization of fossil fuels, humans became amazingly effective at countering diseases, altering food and water supplies, and in general thwarting nature's every attempt to limit our numbers. The result? Two centuries of dramatic and exponential growth of our population that defies any historical precedent for all of human history's 200,000 years.

Is this unchecked population growth sustainable? Is this but the early stage of growth? Can we continue to grow at this pace? Or have we reached a frothy state? Are there indications of a bubble?

I am a businessman; I am analytical. I was taught to look at and question facts and figures. I also learned in graduate school that, "You can't manage what you can't measure." I learned an even more important lesson from an ecologist: "You must measure what you treasure."

To get to the heart of the issue, we are outstripping our planet's resources and emitting waste faster than the earth can regenerate those resources or absorb those wastes. Our planet is sick and it is showing us in numerous ways.

Two of the most evident and poignant examples are the annual loss of natural habitat equivalent to the size of Ireland and the related loss of the creatures that inhabited these lands. WWF measurements of 3,706 vertebrate species show an astounding worldwide decline of more than half their total population numbers since the 1970s.

Attempt after attempt at curtailing resource use, whether by improved technology or voluntarily trying to reduce our consumption, has failed simply because of our desire to live better lives compounded with our growth in numbers. Every day we add 220,000 more people to the planet. That translates to 80 million more people each year. By 2023, only six years from now, there will be 8 billion people requiring food, water, clothing, and shelter. Most will also expect dependable electricity, transportation, and a whole host of additional goods and services. At 8 billion people, each person will roughly be allocated only 4 acres of land for all their resource needs, crowding out ever more of the native plants and animals that once inhabited these lands.

I was shocked to witness so many intelligent leaders in the environmental movement shy away from discussing overpopulation in a responsible manner, preferring to highlight safer, sexier, and more politically correct "solutions" like green energy, recycling, organic farming, and going vegan.

So in 2017 I embarked on a documentary film project to investigate and highlight real people confronting the challenges of living and working with overburdened ecosystems and natural resources.

Real sustainability to reverse devastation shown in this polluted river in India will require a paradigm shift emphasizing a small family ethic, educating and empowering women, promoting family planning, and advocating for a carbon fee and dividend plan.

© *Terry Spahr, Executive Producer,* 8 Billion Angels

Slated for festivals in 2019, our movie, *8 Billion Angels,* crises carries the message that everyone deserves to hear about our crises and the steps that we can all take to address them. Real, achievable sustainability will require a paradigm shift emphasizing a small family ethic, educating and empowering women, promoting family planning, and advocating for a carbon fee and dividend plan.

My hope lies in taking the first step and daring to tell the whole truth about sustainability, and that truth means saying that human numbers matter. They matter a lot. It is time to eliminate the taboos surrounding overpopulation and to embrace the requisite (and long overdue) objective of humanely achieving a healthy population level.

Anyone in the business of making the world a better place needs to understand and spread this message without being afraid of the blowback from those less informed. The alternative—doing nothing—is far more devastating.

This conversation must be broadened, diversified, and amplified if we are going to begin changing the norms and if we are going to choose the path toward a more just, peaceful, and prosperous future for our children and grandchildren.

POETRY

Raven. © *Susan Morgan*

THE GOOD NEWS

BY GARY LAWLESS

Wolf circling the statehouse. © *Susan Morgan*

Roads disappear, and the caribou wander through.
The beaver just gets tired of it, reaches
up, through the ice,
grabs the trapper's feet and
pulls him down.
Wolves come back on their own,
circle the State House,
howl at the Governor and
piss on the ATVs.
Trees grow everywhere.
The machines stop,
and the air is full of birdsong.

THROUGH HIGH STILL AIR

BY TIM MCNULTY

Sourdough Mountain lies at the heart of the North Cascades. A mile above the Skagit River canyon at the intersection of six major drainages, it commands one of the most spectacular views in the range.

The dry summer of 2003 marked a milestone in the cultural history of the mountains. It was the 50th anniversary of poet Gary Snyder's stint as Sourdough Mountain lookout. Gary's tenure in the North Cascades, along with fellow writers Phillip Whalen and Jack Kerouac, was celebrated in John Sutter's 2002 book, *Poets on the Peaks*.

When the park service decided to reactivate Sourdough Mountain Lookout for the remainder of the 2003 fire season and began looking for a fire guard, friends let me know. I jumped at the opportunity. A few days later I was alone amid one of the most spectacular mountain wilderness landscapes in North America.

From *Through High Still Air, A Season at Sourdough Mountain*, Pleasure Boat Studio, New York, 2005

Night, Sourdough Mountain Lookout

A late-summer sun
Threads the needles of McMillan Spires
And disappears in a reef of coral cloud.
Winds roll the mountain trees,
Batter the shutter props.
I light a candle with the coming dark.
Its reflection in the window glass
Flickers over mountains and
Shadowed valleys
Seventeen miles north to Canada.
Not another light.
The lookout is a dim star
Anchored to a rib of the planet
Like a skiff to a shoal
In a wheeling sea of stars.
Night sky at full flood.
Wildly awake.

Looking over Ross Lake to Sourdough from
Desolation Peak. © John Miles

COEXISTENCE

Petroglyph-style Coyote. © *Karen Boeger*

THE SAGA OF THE MEXICAN GRAY WOLF (EL LOBO)

BY DAVE PARSONS, THE REWILDING INSTITUTE

Overzealous predator eradication programs initiated by the federal government in the early 1900s were effective in killing all Mexican gray wolves (*Canis lupus baileyi*; aka Lobos) in the wild throughout their entire historic range in the southwestern United States and Mexico by the early 1980s. The Endangered Species Act was passed in the nick of time to save the lobos, the southernmost and most genetically distinct subspecies of gray wolf (*Canis lupus*) in North America, from certain extinction.

Mexican wolves once roamed the US Southwest and northern Mexico by the thousands. An exact population estimate is impossible. Wherever there was prey, there were Mexican wolves. Wherever there was adequate moisture and available forage and water sources, there was prey. The best habitat was generally the mid to high elevations in the mountainous regions and the riparian zones along rivers and streams.

Mexican wolves are the smallest subspecies of gray wolves in North America, rarely exceeding 80 pounds for large males. Females are 15 to 20 pounds lighter. Some scientists believe that the epicenter of evolution for the Mexican wolf subspecies was in the Sierra Madres of northern Mexico and Sky Islands region of the southwestern United States in southern Arizona and New Mexico. The principal prey in this region was the diminutive Coues whitetail deer—rarely exceeding 100 pounds—and other prey species were likely javelina (collared peccary), coatimundi, beavers, jackrabbits, cottontails, and other small mammals.

The prevailing hypothesis is that Mexican wolves evolved to have smaller body size because of the smaller size of prey available and because of the need to shed more heat in the warm climate of the region. The latter phenomenon is known as Bergmann's Rule. Nineteenth century German biologist Carl Bergmann observed that within species with broad distributions over a north-south gradient, those in the colder climes have larger bodies than those in the warmer climes. The theory is that a warm-blooded animal's body-surface-to-volume ratio is important in regulating body temperature by either retaining (smaller surface-to-volume ratio in large bodied animals) or dissipating (larger surface-to-volume ratio in small bodied animals) heat. This phenomenon holds true for many wide-ranging species.

As gray wolves radiated across North America from their entry point at the eastern end of the Bering Strait to their southern-most distribution near the latitude of Mexico City, they evolved and adapted to the variety of climatic and ecological conditions they encountered. Historically, gray wolves were contiguously distributed from the Arctic to Mesoamerica. Variations among subspecies were subtle rather than abrupt, with fuzzy boundaries between the subspecies taxonomists described. But wolves living substantial distances apart along this distribution exhibited measurable physical, genetic, and ecological differences.

Mexican wolves at the northern end of their distribution blended into populations that were somewhat larger and preyed on the abundant Merriam's elk and even bison in adjacent regions. That Mexican wolves reintroduced into the Gila region prey primarily on the transplanted Rocky Mountain elk—Merriam's elk having been shot to extinction in the early 20th century—is a testament to their evolutionary plasticity.

As European settlers moved west with their large herds of livestock beginning in the late 1800s, two problems occurred

*The future of lobos in the Southwest depends on relentless pressure
applied to responsible state and federal agencies and elected
officials by dedicated citizen activists, conservation organizations,
independent scientists, and conservation-oriented lawyers.
Wolf. © Robin Silver Photography*

simultaneously to permanently alter our Southwestern ecosystems. Unregulated hunting for sport and markets decimated wildlife populations. And unregulated grazing by cattle and sheep degraded fragile grasslands and riparian ecosystems. Watersheds were laid bare and erosion was unleashed with a vengeance blighting landscapes to a condition that the ecologically unenlightened now perceive as the normal "look" of the West.

The early western cattle barons were politically connected, and convinced Congress to pass legislation to establish a federal agency in 1915 with a mission of eradicating large predators from the land.

Mexican wolves narrowly escaped extinction with the passage of the Endangered Species Act in 1973 and their placement on the list of endangered species in 1976. A few wild Mexican wolves remained in the remote Sierra Madre in the Mexican states of Chihuahua, Sonora, and Durango. A renowned Texas trapper named Roy McBride was hired in 1977 to live-trap as many wild Lobos as possible in Mexico. Between 1977 and 1980 he trapped five wild Mexican wolves—four males and one pregnant female. These were placed in captive breeding facilities in the United States and became the "certified" lineage of Mexican wolves for purposes of captive breeding for future reintroduction to their former wild habitats. Only the female and one of the captured males reproduced in captivity. Counting the wild uncaptured mate of the pregnant female, this breeding line stems from three founders.

Concerns over the limited gene pool led to the testing of two additional captive lineages of Mexican wolves, called the Ghost Ranch and Aragon lines. A team of canid geneticists using new molecular genetic and traditional morphological methods determined in 1995 that both of these lines were pure Mexican wolves. This increased the number of founders for the captive population to seven wolves—three females and four males. All of the approximately 400 Mexican wolves alive today in both captivity and the wild can be traced to these seven founders.

Following many years of captive breeding and lengthy analyses and public reviews, the first Lobos were released into the Apache National Forest in eastern Arizona in 1998. More than 100 Mexican wolves have been released up to the present day; and the current wild population inhabiting suitable habitats in Arizona and New Mexico is estimated to be a minimum of 114 Lobos. More recent releases in Mexico have resulted in a current wild population there hovering around 30 wolves.

The wild populations of Mexican wolves face serious threats to their long-term survival. Responsible wildlife agencies need to confront these threats for Lobos to regain population levels that would allow them to be removed from the list of endangered species. The two main threats are limited genetic diversity and excessive human-caused mortality. State wildlife agencies have pressured the U.S. Fish and Wildlife Service to limit releases of genetically valuable animals from the captive population. The current wild population has a very high inbreeding coefficient which can lead to genetic problems potentially affecting their long-term survival. And the combination of illegal killing and management-related removal of wolves has slowed recovery. Few poachers have been prosecuted for illegally killing Mexican wolves.

Recent revisions of the federal rules for managing the wild population and of the official Mexican Wolf Recovery Plan reflect political influences driven by state wildlife regulatory bodies (game commissions), which are disproportionately influenced by hunters and ranchers. Pressure from New Mexico, Arizona, Utah, and Colorado governors and wildlife managers has resulted in too few Mexican wolves required for removal from the list of endangered species, limited options for releasing wolves from the more genetically diverse captive population, and set a politically motivated northern limit for Mexican wolf occupation at Interstate 40 in Arizona and New Mexico. The Endangered Species Act requires recovery decisions to be based on the best available science, not politics.

Conservation plaintiffs recently won a lawsuit when a federal district court judge ruled that decisions made in the 2015 Mexican wolf management rule were "arbitrary and capricious" and not based on the best available science. The Judge has ordered the U.S. Fish and Wildlife Service to revise the rule in accordance with requirements of the Endangered Species Act. This provides an opportunity to improve the chances for the long-term survival of Mexican wolves in the wild.

Early in 2018, two lawsuits were filed on behalf of conservation plaintiffs challenging the legal and scientific sufficiency of the 2017 revised Mexican Wolf Recovery Plan. That plan was developed in closed sessions between representatives of the four southwestern states, wildlife agencies in Mexico, and the Fish and Wildlife Service. The previous recommendations of independent scientists appointed by the Fish and Wildlife Service to a Mexican Wolf Recovery Team formed in late 2010 were rejected by the states and subsequently by the Fish and Wildlife Service.

It can be fairly stated that virtually every major advance in the recovery of Mexican wolves has been forced by lawsuits filed by conservation groups; and virtually every decision made by the U.S. Fish and Wildlife Service has been influenced by the politics of special interests antithetical to the recovery of the Lobos, especially by the southwestern states and their Game and Fish Departments and Commissions. Lobos' long-term well-being will require reforming wildlife management agencies, as well as protecting and expanding the wolves' recovery habitat.

WILDLIFE GOVERNANCE REFORM: WHERE TO BEGIN

BY KIRK ROBINSON, WESTERN WILDLIFE
CONSERVANCY & DAVE PARSONS, THE
REWILDING INSTITUTE

In recent years it has become increasingly obvious that state wildlife governance needs significant reform—in all states, some more than others.

There are three pervasive problems. One is that state wildlife management agencies and their associated wildlife commissions are held captive by special interests—primarily hunting and fishing, livestock, and energy interests. As a consequence, the rightful interests of the majority of citizens are often ignored, and so is scientific knowledge when it is perceived as an obstacle to special interests' objectives. Wildlife populations are being managed less on an ecological model and more on a farm model, with some species being favored and others (typically predators) disfavored. Ironically, this dereliction of public trust duty is viewed by wildlife agencies and their politically appointed commissions as an obligation owed to the special interests.

Another problem is an increasing tendency for federal land management agencies to abrogate their wildlife trust responsibilities in deference to state demands. If a state wildlife management agency wants to transplant an exotic species into a wilderness area or stymie the recovery of an endangered species, the federal government is increasingly willing to step aside and allow it to happen. In fact, Interior Secretary Ryan Zinke is actively working to reverse federal supremacy over state wildlife governance where regulations conflict.[1]

Yet a third problem is that hunting is on the decline throughout the United States, resulting in less money from hunting licenses, and from federal excise taxes on hunting hardware, to support wildlife management programs. Consequently, the agencies are experiencing increased pressure to find new sources of money. Rather than embracing the "nonconsumptive" interests of the larger public, they have instead chosen retrenchment, as illustrated by creative attempts to recruit young people and women into the hunting culture and by inventing new hunts. One of the more extreme examples of this is Arizona Game & Fish Department co-sponsoring the "Arizona Small Game Challenge," requiring a registration fee of $25 that will be matched by the Sun Chapter of Quail Forever.[2]

Among the numerous examples that illustrate the first two problems in tandem is the story of how a single sheep rancher has been allowed to retain three grazing allotments in the 500,000-acre Weminuche Wilderness of Colorado's San Juan Mountains, despite the threat his sheep pose to the small herd of native bighorn sheep. This herd, numbering fewer than 500 animals, is in serious danger of contracting a lethal disease from the domestic sheep. If this happens, it will likely decimate the wild herd and may wipe it out entirely. Nevertheless, the Colorado Department of Parks and Wildlife, abetted by the Colorado Wildlife Commission and the U.S. Forest Service, is determined to keep this one 66-year old rancher in business at all costs. They promise to kill any bighorn sheep that "strays" too close to the domestic sheep when they are in the wilderness.[3]

This scenario is being duplicated repeatedly, with variations, in many states across the nation. In Utah, the U.S. Forest Service allowed the Utah Division of Wildlife Resources to transplant non-native Rocky Mountain goats into the Manti-La Sal National Forest in the mountains east of Moab for the purpose of trophy

Majestic bighorns like these deserve ecological management and protection to ensure the integrity, stability, and beauty of biotic communities. © Kirk Robinson

hunting. There is a Research Natural Area in the alpine zone that is sure to be negatively impacted by the exotic creatures. The Forest Service had the authority to prevent the project from going forward in order to protect the RNA. Instead, the Forest Service chose to merely voice opposition to the project at the last minute. Now the goats have become established, and scientific monitoring has shown that they are wreaking havoc on the fragile alpine zone and its endemic plant species. This has become the subject of litigation by the Grand Canyon Trust and other conservation organizations.

One of the most egregious examples of state demands cowing the federal government has been the states of Arizona, New Mexico, Colorado, and Utah teaming up to effectively thwart recovery of the highly endangered Mexican gray wolf, the most ancient subspecies of gray wolf and one of the mostly highly endangered mammals in North America. After twenty years of half-hearted recovery effort, there are still barely more than one hundred Mexican wolves in the wild in the United States. This struggling population descended from seven founders and is severely genetically inbred. Independent science experts have determined that without more captive wolves released into the wild in more places, including southwest Colorado and the greater Grand Canyon region, it is nearly certain that this subspecies of wolf will slowly go extinct. Why is this being allowed to happen? Because the state governments are hell-bent on protecting certain hunting and livestock interests and view full recovery of the Mexican wolf as a threat to those interests. And because the U.S. Fish and Wildlife Service has chosen to bow to the politically motivated interests of the states rather than do its job, as mandated by the Endangered Species Act.

Power and authority are not identical. The federal government has supreme authority over state wildlife management, particularly as concerns threatened and endangered species and as concerns federal lands such as Forest Service and BLM lands. State governors typically have the authority to appoint wildlife commissioners, and in most cases state statutes allow them to appoint commissioners who are free from ties to consumptive interests. The problem is that the interests in support of consumptive wildlife use have a lot of power because they have a lot of money and they support each other. As a bloc, they are able to exert tremendous influence over the election process to get the governors and legislators they want—and through them, the wildlife commissioners they want. This in turn is resulting in tremendous pushback against federal agencies.

This problem has become so acute that wildlife conservationists recently decided they must do something about it. The result was a first of its kind conference held in Albuquerque in mid-August: "Wildlife for All: Re-envisioning State Wildlife Governance." The idea is to re-envision state wildlife governance and work to transform it. The conference was organized by the Southwest Environmental Center in Las Cruces with assistance by Western Wildlife Conservancy in Salt Lake City. By all accounts, the national conference was a huge success, with more than 100 people from 21 states attending and participating.

The opening talk by Kevin Bixby, Executive Director of the Southwest Environmental Center, laid the groundwork for the conference by presenting an overview of the problem and how it arose. This was followed by reports from various states, including New Mexico, California, and New Hampshire. Next there was an expert panel discussion on the public trust doctrine as a legal framework for bringing about change (including a critique of the so-called "North American Model of Wildlife Conservation"). Subsequent panels discussed lessons learned from recent successful campaigns, the politics of change (including building alliances with sportsmen), possible alternative funding sources for wildlife conservation, reconstituting state wildlife commissions to better serve the public and wildlife, and last but not least, the ingredients necessary for building a movement that will culminate in reform. In his keynote address, Mike Phillips (career wildlife biologist and current Montana state senator) urged concerned conservationists to embrace politics as a means to effect change and run for public office. Closing remarks by Kirk Robinson, Executive Director of Western Wildlife Conservancy, focused on beauty as an intrinsic value of wild animals and ecosystems.

We hope the "Wildlife for All" conference will prove to be a watershed event. Here are some things that you can do to help reform wildlife governance.

- Join or form a coalition in your state to implement wildlife governance reform;
- Run for public office;
- Advocate for legal reforms that affirm your state's public trust responsibility to all wildlife for all citizens;
- Attend meetings of your state Wildlife (Game) Commission and insist that their decisions embrace the views of all interest groups and are based on sound science—not political pressure from special interests;
- Urge your Governor to appoint qualified experts to the Wildlife Commission.

Reforming wildlife governance at both state and federal levels will not be easy, but it is a challenge we must embrace with zeal for the sake of our national wildlife heritage.

---

1 www.sltrib.com/news/nation-world/2018/09/11/zinke-seeks-more-state/
2 www.azgfd.com/azgfd-invites-hunters-to-take-arizona-small-game-challenge/
3 www.hcn.org/issues/50.15/wildlife-agricultural-interests-steer-colorados-wildlife-management

FOSTERING WILDLIFE-FRIENDLY FARMING AND RECOGNIZING BIODIVERSITY AS CRITICAL TO A FULLY FUNCTIONING FARM

BY JO ANN BAUMGARTNER, WILD FARM ALLIANCE

We support what is beautiful and what we love—songbirds singing out their names, fat bumblebees busy sampling an array of gorgeous native flowers, and the majestic oaks towering over us—these animals and plants can and do live on farms. Are they what make a farm beautiful?

There's a debate raging here and especially in Europe where eco-payments are made to farmers to protect rare species. It goes like this: Should we have agricultural sacrificial zones separate from protected wild places, or should we have wildlife-friendly farms? The sacrificial zones are where the crop is grown fencerow to fencerow and every other plant is killed with herbicides or fire, and livestock are confined to small areas and are not allowed to graze. The Wild Farm Alliance (wildfarmalliance.org) maintains that from every perspective—beauty, functionality, and biodiversity—we must have both large protected areas and wildlife-friendly matrices.

Agriculture occupies almost 60% of the contiguous United States and 40% of the Earth's landscape. As our population grows and our planet heats up, it is imperative that we recognize the benefits biodiversity provides—particularly, pollination, pest control, clean water, and fertile soils. These biodiversity benefits can help the farm be more resilient to changes in climate that will cause increasing drought, heat waves, and floods. Among the most important components of biodiversity, natural predators help control pests and diseases, and help prevent over-browsing of plant communities. A biologically diverse farm, then, is addressing the global extinction crisis.

In my mind, a beautiful farm is one where the farmer makes a living not just on the land, but also from the diversity of the natural world. In so doing, that farmer has a richer experience interacting with nature (as opposed to solely growing corn and soybeans, over and over), and ultimately, supports wild nature.

Take a walk with me through a few diversified farms in the Central Coast of California. Let's start at Live Earth Farm. The songbirds are now singing every morning because it is breeding season—the insectivorous ones, like Chestnut-backed Chickadees, are eating codling moth, so the proverbial worm that would have been in the apple instead helps to feed their young. The oak trees that are interspersed throughout the farm (especially on steeper slopes that aren't tilled) support up to 5,000 insect species—500 of which are caterpillars in their larval stage—big food sources for nestlings. While worldwide honeybees (a species introduced from Eurasia) are in decline, native bees are helping to take up the slack, especially on this farm where conserved native habitat provides nectar and pollen and nesting sites—hollow stems for tunnel-nesting bees and open ground for ground-nesting bees. Corridors for wildlife movement are protected on the farm. Come summer, the apricots are to die for, the tomatoes exquisite, and a multitude of other produce, amazing. As these crops bloom, they are giving back to the pollinators and beneficial insects, supporting some of their food needs.

Of course, there are trade-offs to coexistence with nature. For instance, the errant chicken that escaped its electrically fenced

Songbirds like the Chestnut-backed Chickadee (Poecile rufenscens)
thrive on wildlife-friendly farms. © *Dave Foreman*

yard has become food for a bobcat. Regional studies suggest that the birds farmers tend to see as pests (the non-insect-eating kind) consume about as many strawberries as the insectivorous birds save by eating the strawberry's pest insects. Even with the trade-offs, the farm is viable and highly successful.

Strolling through Phil Foster's Ranch, we see crop diversity as varied as Live Earth Farm's, but it is more in the flatlands where there are fewer wild corridors and edges. Nevertheless, a restored riparian area stabilizes the riverbanks and helps support wide-ranging predators that keep rodents in check; and huge native plant hedgerows support beneficial native bees and natural enemy insects and birds. The riparian corridor and the hedgerows also store woody carbon. Tradeoffs are managed with specific techniques. For example, the farmers plant the first few rows adjacent to one hedgerow with crops that aren't attractive to pest birds; and use temporary fencing along another hedgerow when the crop is young to discourage foraging of the crop by the quail that have taken up residence in the hedgerow. In the end, the produce is as delicious as you can find—roast their flavorful bell peppers, caramelize their big red onions, steam their flat Italian green beans, eat their fresh cherries...

Our trail takes us to Morris Grassfed Beef's operation where pasture-raised cattle graze on thousands of acres. Their holistically managed animals are rotated through the landscape to allow high quality forage, carbon sequestration in the soil, and maintenance of biodiversity. Wide-ranging wildlife such as mountain lions, coyotes, black-tailed deer, and hawks also use these landscapes. The cattle are treated with care which comes through in the meat—it is succulent, bite after bite, and good for you with higher amounts of beta-carotene, vitamin E and omega-3 fatty acids than beef produced using conventional cattle-feeding strategies. By never allowing the animals to overgraze, the ranchers maintain more vegetation in creeks and riparian areas. They are seeing more native than non-native grasses; and shrubs are retained, to support birds like the Scrub Jay. The Scrub Jay is a restoration specialist, burying more acorns than it can find later, thereby fostering oak regeneration. If there is a trade off to such holistic livestock management, it is that rotational grazing is more labor intensive than just turning out the cattle—and letting them graze, and graze, until they overgraze the landscape.

The last stop takes us through Deep Roots Ranch, a heritage breed operation raising cows, chickens, turkeys, and sheep. Even on smaller acreage, Deep Roots Ranch shows that farms can be integrated with nature. The secret to their success is that they are grass farmers—keeping the pasture healthy means matching the number of animals to what the grass can support. They've restored a muddy ditch back into a clear running creek through the middle of their property, supporting numerous songbirds and aquatic species. How many ways can you cook lamb? A fun and delicious way to find out is by purchasing an animal from Deep Roots.

Drive through other agricultural areas and you will see very different farming practices. Row crops are grown with "clean" edges and orchards with cleared understories where they could have supported pollinators and natural enemy insects—instead, these farms pay extra for pollination (beehives) and pest control (pesticides or beneficial insect releases). Animals are set apart from their natural food sources in small pens. If they are on pastures or rangeland, they are spread out on overgrazed land instead of moving through in tight groups (an evolutionary tactic for safety from predators). These conventional farms have a long way to go toward better ecosystem functionality provided by biodiversity.

Farmers can diversify their operations through various wildlife-friendly practices. Research from UC Berkeley is confirming that diversified farming systems progress and support the farm along a simple to complex continuum—from mixed cropping and livestock systems, cover crops, and hedgerows to riparian corridors on the farm and natural landscapes surrounding the farm. Wild Farm Alliance has identified several steps focusing on plant diversity that support biological diversity along the continuum:

- Rotate crops, and plant cover crops and pastures to support diverse microorganisms in the rhizosphere.
- Keep the soil covered with a crop, pasture plants, or non-invasive plants as much as possible. Plant a cover crop understory in perennial crops. Allow non-invasive plants to grow along fencerows and in ditches.
- Manage plant pests without using pesticides that harm pollinators, beneficial insects, reptiles, amphibians, birds, bats, or other mammals.
- Provide nectar and pollen by planting annual non-invasive sequentially flowering plants interspersed through the crop, at the ends of crop rows, and in pastures.
- Plant native flowering buffer strips, hedgerows, and perennial understories for native plant-eating insects (frogs, lizards, birds, and mammals all rely on these as food sources).
- Increase food, cover, and nesting sites by planting and conserving structural and compositional diversity of native trees, shrubs, forbs, and grasses on crop perimeters and interspersed through pastures.
- Create native plant corridors to connect with natural habitat patches and pastures on the farm and with larger natural areas off the farm. Support watershed level restoration.
- Conserve and restore grasslands, shrublands, woodlands, wetlands, and riparian areas, especially habitats of the highest conservation value that support rare species.

As more farmers use these kinds of diversified farming practices, we will have a mosaic of food production areas that get better and better at providing valuable ecosystem benefits.

Food makes us who we are, from our earliest remembrances of how a raspberry tasted, to what was served at an important celebration in our lives. Gastronomists believe we enjoy our food more when we identify with its origin—for example, people rate their enjoyment of eating shellfish higher when they are listening to sounds of the ocean.

Times are changing for food and farming. So many more people are paying attention to cooking shows and questioning where their food comes from. Much of that attention is focused on buying local and pesticide-free food. Local is about eating fresh food and supporting your human neighbors, and pesticide reduction means we and the many species that share this planet are less impacted by toxins. These actions are important, but not enough.

Food and farming embody more than that—they are about supporting the beauty and functionality that biodiversity provides on the farm. Diverse farming systems support our wild neighbors and the ecosystem. If you like eating that local pesticide-free apple, you just might love eating one that grew with native bees buzzing in its flowers, songbirds serenading and keeping it safe from pests, and creeks murmuring by. If farmers could share the sounds of nature from their farms, it would undoubtedly widen the enjoyment and support for their food. Consumers, farmers, and ecologists are helping to evolve the food and farming movement to a new level—one that goes beyond organic to incorporate biodiversity in our world. Support beautiful farms along the biodiversity continuum!

For a copy of *How to Conserve Biodiversity on the Farm: Actions to Take on a Continuum from Simple to Complex*, go to wildfarmalliance.org/biodiversity_continuum.

BOWMAN DIVIDE CRITTER CROSSING

BY BRAD MEIKLEJOHN

My father, Jim Meiklejohn, founded the Randolph Conservation Commission and served as its chairman for nearly two decades before passing away in 2014. One of his long held goals was to see the construction of a "critter crossing" at Bowman Divide along U.S. Route 2 in Randolph, New Hampshire. Such a wildlife corridor would logically connect the large expanses of National Forest to the south of Route 2 with the Randolph Town Forest and the Kilkenny portion of the National Forest to the north.

Wildlife of all kinds cross Route 2 in the Bowman area to get to the other side. Moose, deer, black bears, coyotes, beaver, and bobcats are common, and even lynx have been documented crossing the road. If we don't see them live, we find them at the end of a trail of black skidmarks. Roads are a hazard to wildlife, and wildlife are a hazard to people on the roads.

There are alternatives to good timing and bad luck. Around the world, highways have been retrofitted with bridges and tunnels that save the lives of people and animals.

Wildlife crossing structures have been built in many countries and in many parts of North America to benefit species ranging from elk, bear, cougar, bison, and moose to rare mice and snakes. On a recent trip through Idaho, Nevada, Utah, and Arizona, I saw thousands of these structures, mostly simple underpasses with fencing to channel wildlife to the crossing location.

Wildlife overpasses and underpasses work and are effective at reducing collisions that threaten people and animals. So far, no large wildlife crossing structures have been built in the

*A partial antidote to the fragmentation of natural ecosystems is the
construction on busy roads of safe wildlife crossings, overpasses and
underpasses, with fences to funnel animals to these safe passages.*
© Sheri Amsel, exploringnature.org

northeastern U.S., but the benefits to motorists and wildlife would be the same here as elsewhere in the world.

The principal benefits of the Bowman Divide location are:

- Conserved lands abut U.S. Route 2 immediately to the north and south.
- Wildlife use and crossings of Route 2 have been well-documented.
- Vehicle/wildlife collisions are common in this area and are a serious threat to travelers and interstate commerce.
- A critter crossing at Bowman Divide or a similar location would be a North Country attraction and would set a new standard for road design/construction in the Northeast.

The idea of a critter crossing at Bowman Divide has been studied extensively over the years by the New Hampshire Department of Transportation (NHDOT), New Hampshire Fish and Game, and New Hampshire Audubon; and specific sites have been identified along this section of Route 2 where wildlife road crossings are particularly concentrated. NHDOT considered the construction of a critter crossing at the Bowman Divide location during its planning efforts when the highway was realigned in 2007.

The Environmental Impact Study for that project noted that at Bowman Divide "the natural terrain on the north side of the roadway funnels wildlife to this area, making it an ideal location for a crossing, enabling access to protected natural lands to the north and south." While NHDOT found the idea had merit based on wildlife activity and likely would reduce vehicle collisions, they ultimately did not include a critter crossing in their designs when the highway was realigned in 2007. At that time, NHDOT estimated the costs for an underpass crossing at the Bowman Divide location to be in the range of $250,000 to $350,000.

In addition to the Bowman location, large culverts at sites just west of the Mount Jefferson Motel in western Randolph and at Stag Hollow Brook near the junction of NH Route 115 and U.S.

2 could easily be adapted with minimal cost to serve as effective critter crossings.

In 2016, New Hampshire State Senator David Watters sponsored and passed Senate Bill 376, An Act Relative to Wildlife Corridors, in the New Hampshire State Legislature. This legislation was initially focused specifically on encouraging state agencies to advance critter crossings on U.S. Route 2 but was ultimately broadened to facilitate the construction of wildlife crossings throughout New Hampshire.

Before my father died, he asked that we "do something green" for him. His proposed critter crossing at Bowman Divide is an idea whose time has come. Randolph has been a trailblazer in land conservation through an innovative and extensive town forest. A critter crossing at Bowman would allow wildlife to move between the Town Forest and national forest more easily and more safely for them and us. Let's break this trail to save the lives of people and wildlife.

WANTED:
MISSING CAT

Have You Seen This Cat? Neither Have We.

Puma. © Susan Morgan

Because sadly, these beautiful creatures have been missing from the East for a very long time, in fact, a lifetime.

Now it's time to bring the cougars back home.

Back to our wild preserves: such as Adirondack Park, Green Mountain National Forest, Okefenokee National Wildlife Refuge, Monongahela National Forest, Great Smoky Mountains National Park, and Shenandoah National Park.

Before it's too late.

The truth is, these natural predators and amazing athletes can help save your life. But only if you help save theirs.

Talk to your neighbors; pressure your state and federal wildlife agencies; ask them to help restore cougars to their rightful homes their wild preserves. For balance, for love of the wilds, for life.

For more information on how to help restore this missing cat to its rightful home, see rewilding.org or CougarRewilding.org

Go, Wild.

BY SHERRY NEMMERS, CREATIVE CONCEPT, WRITER

Brand designer Sherry Nemmers and Rewilding Earth invite carnivore advocates to copy and post this bulletin or create their own, on behalf of missing native cats and dogs. **See and download the original bulletin at rewilding.org/cat.**

THE KILLING ROADS

BY SANDRA COVENY, FREELANCE WRITER,
CLIMATE ADAPTATION ACTIVIST

"Looking at life from a different perspective makes you realize that it's not the deer that is crossing the road, rather it's the road that is crossing the forest."

—MUHAMMAD ALI

Over one million animals will die on US roads today. Over one million animals will die on roads in Brazil today. Half a million rare and endangered animals, like the ones you visit in zoos, will die on the roads in Tasmania this year. Over a hundred animals, such as deer, panthers, tigers, armadillos, porcupines, squirrels, Tasmanian devils, raccoons, and eagles will be killed by cars in the US, India, and Brazil combined by the time you are done reading this article. The list goes on, and would be much worse if we considered the billions of small creatures, particularly flying insects, killed by cars every year. That is more wildlife deaths by roads and motor vehicles than by poachers, deforestation, or pollution (Brazil, 2018). And now we are learning that there may be links between increasing roadkill numbers and the impacts of climate change. The results of carbon emissions include changing the timing and availability of both food and water—for humans (Quaempts, 2018) and for wildlife (see Sweden case study below). For both humans and wildlife, that change means traveling farther and wider in search of food and water; and for wildlife, it means risking death by crossing more roads, with more frequency.

Since humans began using means other than foot travel, there have been casualties due to collisions. My great uncle was

*Roads and associated vehicles are the biggest threats to wildlife
across North America and most of the over-developed world.*
© *Sheri Amsel, exploringnature.org*

killed by a horse and cart in Poland when he was a child. Many people and domestic animals (dogs, cats, chickens, goats) were struck and killed or maimed on narrow streets by passing horses and their drawn carts. Since the modern car became commonplace around the globe, starting in the 1920s, there has been increasing roadkill. Today, with nearly 8 billion people on the planet driving 1.2 billion cars (Volker, J. 2014) and with the impacts of climate change on water and food availability approaching a nadir, cars and roads are becoming the single most dangerous threat facing wildlife (arguably, all life) today.

People have taken many steps and spent millions of dollars to save lives of the humans driving and riding in cars, and other potential human victims of the automobile. We have crosswalks, crossing lights, pedestrian rights of way, seat belts, airbags, auto-braking technology, backup lights, back up beepers, and drivers' education—which is a series of videos showing gruesome accidents, aimed at scaring new drivers into compliance with safety rules of the road.

When animal-vehicle conflicts are mentioned, it is most often in the context of monetary cost: damages to your car, insurance claims, and hospital bills. In New England, for example, it's common to see a bright yellow sign with a moose outline and the words: "Brake for Moose: It could save your life." But what about the moose?

The spiritual toll for our fossil fuel addiction runs deep: nature deficit disorder is very real (Louv, 2005), and is the result of a fracture between our need to connect with nature and our realities of living separate from it. Cars are the most obvious and the most personal manifestation of both our addiction to fossil fuels and our disconnect from the earth and its other inhabitants. By driving cars, we isolate ourselves from experiencing the place through which we travel. Instead of experiencing the time as distance travelled, smells and tactile experiences, and yes, even pain and exhaustion, we career around in a controlled and tiny environment, listening to stories or music, missing out on the sounds and smells and experience of the place. At the same time as we isolate ourselves in cars from each other and from other animals, we are contributing up to 20% of the total global greenhouse gas emissions through driving.

Another toll taken is the psychological impact of killing something by mistake and seeing dead animals splayed out, often gory, along the roads. Sure, there are those few deliberate killers who speed up in order to hit the target in the road; and oppositely, there are those few who get out and try to move a fellow creature out of the road (e.g. turtles). More of us, though, are just quietly diminished by the ongoing tragedy of roadkill. Anyone who has lost a person, dog, or cat to a car collision remembers the trauma well. Those who have hit and killed anything with their car— and who among us has not?!—know that life is never the same afterward. Roadkill is inconvenient, expensive, and hazardous— and it also can deplete one's spirit and cause lasting emotional trauma. Conversely, taking action to report and reduce these needless and traumatic experiences can serve as a healing balm on many levels.

Case Studies

I wanted to know which countries suffer the highest roadkill numbers and to learn what they are doing about reducing those numbers and how well different remedies are working. I looked at the data about roadkill, including the sources of funding for studies where data were collected. Many roadkill studies are conducted by insurance companies because of the resulting insurance claims by drivers of cars damaged after collisions with large wildlife. I did not focus on those studies because their data are not comprehensive—and they generally do not document smaller animals such as birds, rodents, reptiles, and amphibians.

I narrowed my investigation to countries with abundant roadkill data, where roadkill studies were done in service to preservation of biodiversity, and with the exception of Sweden, to places where CO2 emissions are among the highest levels globally. These countries have abundant data from credible sources, and have a high potential to set examples that could change global behavior:

Sweden - their studies cited climate change as one of the reasons for increased roadkill;

India - high biodiversity and the country contributes 6% of the global CO2 emissions;

Brazil - considered the country with the highest biodiversity and also contributes 1% of the global CO2 emissions;

United States - high biodiversity, and contributes 16% of the global CO2 emissions.

Roadkill is exacerbated by many factors, I looked for information regarding each of the following causes for roadkill and related solutions:

Ignorance - Either during the road design process where wildlife needs were overlooked in the first place, or by drivers not paying close attention, or by the animals not being road savvy.

External pressures - Habitat loss and degradation caused by human impacts can force animal migration patterns to change.

Attraction to carrion of other wildlife - Many collisions are the result of the first roadkill becoming food for the next.

Climate Change - While this can be considered a habitat constraint, I kept it separate because it's an important but often overlooked habitat constraint. Because of climate change, animals are turning up in areas where they are not expected and where road conditions are not conducive to wildlife crossing.

Sweden

Sweden has spent significant resources to protect animals from roads. And they are spending more as a result of a recently documented sharp increase in roadkill. According to multiple sources in Sweden's media, 2016 saw the highest number of automobile-animal collisions, up 20%—which represents the sharpest rise in their history of documenting roadkill. Wildlife biologists state that this increase is due to changes in wildlife behaviors and travel patterns as a result of the effects of climate change. According to the Swedish news source *The Local:*

"A warmer climate is believed to be the main reason behind the increase [in road kill], with mild winters and dry spells in summer causing the animals to travel longer distances in search of water."

The problem compounds when the animals who scavenge roadkill are killed by cars while trying to eat the carcasses. Sweden's eagles are suffering the most as a result of the increased occurrences of roadkill. The increase in dead moose, deer, and reindeer is creating a veritable buffet for carrion eaters, especially those opportunistic critters who prefer to not have to kill for themselves, like eagles. Last year (2017), "a total of 96 eagles were killed in traffic, as were 33 lynx, 12 bears, six wolves and two wolverines." Eagles. Being killed by cars. That should say it all.

Their solutions: Remove roadkill off the roads more quickly to reduce the secondary kills; and repair and lengthen fences where roadkill is most prevalent.

Brazil

Brazil is one of the most biologically diverse countries in the world. Recognizing that, its people have taken on the task of understanding the impacts of roadkill and how to reduce them. Brazil estimates that upwards of 1 million animals are killed every day on their roads.

In 2011, Brazilian ecologists launched an app for smartphones that tracks roadkill in real time and helps to inform conservationists and transportation officials about where the problems exist and for which species (*News Atlas*).

In what is currently the most widely cited paper about reducing roadkill in Brazil, Jochen Jaeger, associate professor of geography at Concordia University, conducted a comprehensive study with an international team of ecologists. Their results indicate that a combination of fencing and crossing structures, including culverts, underpasses, and overpasses, were the most effective forms of roadkill prevention. According to the study:

"Of the more than 40 prevention methods available, the researchers found that, overall, fences, with or without crossing structures, reduce roadkill by 54 percent, when considering all species combined. Crossing structures had no detectable effect without fencing.
When large mammals were examined, the combination of fences and crossing structures led to a roadkill reduction of 83 percent, while animal detection systems (such as laser tripwires or radar), led to a 57 per cent reduction." (JAEGER, J. ET AL. 2017)

India

India has been recovering its national animal, the Bengal tiger, aggressively since 1972. Several large reserves have been dedicated to tiger conservation. Also, while much research has been conducted to track movements of tigers through their reserves, several other studies track the populations of other species (such as striped hyenas) in tiger reserves. Roads intersect tiger reserves; and many of the great cats are killed by cars.

One unique effort in India has been the use of tracking collars on tigers for identifying road crossing patterns. GPS is used to map tiger travel routes and habitat uses; so it was a simple matter of using that tracking data to recommend road remediation (Habib, et al 2015).

Tigers are the focus of much research in India, but they are just one of many species of concern; others include hyenas, elephant (full grown animals are killed by trains, and calves are killed by cars and trucks), leopard, Indian civet, and deer. Most carnivore populations are confined to protected areas—which are the last available habitats for these species and are isolated in a sea of human settlements. Many of these reserves actually include human settlements within their boundaries and are bisected by roads, some heavily traveled. As the wildlife populations recover and grow, more animals are leaving reserves and crossing roads.

It's like someone is building a road through your house— your living room is on one side and the kitchen is on the other and if the traffic is continuous, you will feel cutoff from supplies.

This analogy by Sanjay Gubbi, a prominent conservationist in Karnataka, best explains what it is like for wildlife along the 27 km stretch of the Mysore-Mananthwadi Road, which passes through the southern part of the Nagarahole Tiger Reserve.

Researchers at Wildlife Institute of India (WII) looked at travel patterns and roadkill in the Sariska Tiger Reserve in northwestern India. This reserve includes a large population of striped hyenas as well as tigers and other carnivores. The reserve is crossed by two heavily trafficked state highways (No. 13 and 29A). Highway 13 was reported to have around 2,000 vehicles per day. Roadkill accidents were frequent until 2011, when traffic regulations—including night-time highway closures and barriers to divert commercial traffic from areas of frequent roadkill—were enacted. Since then, those studying the impacts of tiger reintroduction on striped hyena populations have noted a significant reduction in tiger and hyena roadkill (Mandal, 2018; Shekhawat, 2013)—in some cases enough to successfully call for permanent sectional road closures.

With research on roadkill, road closures, and road remediation (such as overpasses and underpasses), there are roles for citizen science in data collection. In January of 2018, Wildlife Trust of India and the David Shepherd Wildlife Foundation launched a smartphone app for reporting wildlife sightings or roadkill. The report is geolocated and shared with wildlife managers to help inform the need for continued intervention— from putting up signs to closing major highways to all vehicles *(Mumbai Live)*.

United States

The US has both one of the highest road infrastructure budgets (over $416 billion per year), and among the highest roadkill numbers in the world – estimated at 1 million *vertebrates* run over every day in the U.S., or one every 11.5 seconds (United States Department of Transportation and the Federal Highway Administration). The death toll among other animal groups, especially flying insects, is so huge as to be nearly incalculable.

Collecting roadkill data is a good start. It is not happening universally yet, but there are several examples which you could encourage your state to follow. Understanding where wildlife collisions happen the most is useful, as is knowing what species are being killed at the highest rates. Developing travel corridors in conjunction with fencing and funneling animals into underpasses and onto overpasses is by far the most effective (Simpson et al 2016), but also the most expensive remedy. Short of closing roads and jacking up car prices and associated driving costs (taxes to maintain roads, etc.), installing fences and safe wildlife crossings is the best way to reduce roadkill and lessen the effects of habitat fragmentation.

Since 2009, statewide roadkill observation systems collected tens of thousands of data points from thousands of citizen scientists who are reporting roadkill on smartphones and websites. These sites are educational, and allow you to add your own sightings:

- California Roadkill Observation System (CROS), wildlifecrossing.net/california
- Maine Audubon Wildlife Road Watch, wildlifecrossing.net/maine/
- Idaho Dept. of Fish & Game's Roadkill & Salvage Highway Mortality Reports, idfg.idaho.gov/species/roadkill
- Utah's site was developed by a graduate student who enlisted the help of the state wildlife department. The

app was developed for $34,000—which is not a lot for a state to invest in tracking roadkill. This system is not currently open to citizens and currently only tracks large animals. mapserv.utah.gov/wvc/desktop/index.php

A good overall source of information on road ecology and safe wildlife crossings is the Western Transportation Institute (westerntransportationinstitute.org/programs/road-ecology/). Additional web sources include those of Road Ecology Center, University of California, Davis (roadecology.ucdavis.edu/) and Global Roadkill Network (globalroadkill.net/index.html).

Conclusions

Wildlife put their lives on the line to cross a road and move from one part of their habitat to another for the same reasons humans risk their lives when they become refugees: because THEY HAVE TO. They need food or water or breeding grounds. Across much of the terrestrial world today, wildlife habitats that were connected are now bisected by roads.

You can help reduce the tragedy of roadkill. Support organizations that address this problem—visit globalroadkill. net/org.html_to see if your region is covered. If not, find an organization that will help elevate this issue, especially in areas of high biodiversity. If you see wildlife on the road, alive or dead, report it to someone who will help. Sometimes that is a state wildlife department; sometimes it's a non-profit rescue center.

Our need for transportation is not trivial, but it is among the top causes of death and destruction on the planet. This issue does not change until we demand that change of ourselves and our governments.

Follow up with the resources provided here. In most cases where wildlife crossings have been installed or roads closed, change occurred because someone was devastated by being witness to roadkill. Don't just drive by. Do something.

Citations

Clevenger, A. (2005). Conservation of wildlife crossings: Measures of performance and research directions. Gaia, 14(2), 124-129.

Habib, Bilal, Akanksha Saxena, Indranil Mondal, Asha Rajvanshi, V. B. Mathur and H.S. Negi (2015).

Proposed Mitigation Measures for Maintaining Habitat Contiguity and Reducing Wild Animal Mortality on NH 6 & 7 in the Central Indian Landscape. Technical Report, Wildlife Institute of India, Dehradun and National Tiger Conservation Authority, Govt. of India, New Delhi, pp 100. TR 2015/006.

Herzog, Hal 2010. Road Kill and The New Science of Human-Animal Relationships: Ignore, rescue, or obliterate that turtle in the road? Posted Jul 26, 2010. https://www.psychologytoday.com/us/blog/animals-and-us/201007/road-kill-and-the-new-science-human-animal-relationships

Jaeger, Jochen. 2017. PLos1 https://phys.org/news/2017-04-animals-roadkill.html#jCp

Louv, Richard. 2005. Last Child In The Woods: Saving Our Children From Nature-deficit Disorder. Chapel Hill, NC: Algonquin Books Of Chapel Hill.

Mandal, D. K. (2018). Ecology of striped hyena (Hyaena hyaena) in Sariska Tiger Reserve, Rajasthan. Saurashtra University, Rajkot, Gujarat, India.

Mumbai Live Network. Report Roadkill Anywhere In India With This App. https://www.mumbailive.com/en/tech/report-roadkill-anywhere-in-india-with-roadkill-app-19982

Olson, D.D, Bissonette, J.A., Cramer, P.C., Green, A.D., Davis, S.T., Jackson, P.J., Coster, D.C. Published: June 4, 2014. Monitoring Wildlife-Vehicle Collisions in the Information Age: How Smartphones Can Improve Data Collection PLOS ONE https://journals.plos.org/plosone/article?id=10.1371/journal.pone.0098613

Pasolini, Antonio. News Atlas. Brazilian ecologists launch app to reduce roadkill. Posted April 13, 2014. https://newatlas.com/urubu-app-roadkill/31616/#p264269

Quaempts, Eric J., Krista Jones, Scott J. O'Daniel, Timothy Beechie, Geoffrey C. Poole. 2018. Aligning environmental management with ecosystem resilience: a First Foods example from the Confederated Tribes of the Umatilla Indian Reservation, Oregon, USA. Ecology and Society 23(2):29

Shekhawat, R.S. (2013). Tiger Conservation Plan for Sariska Tiger Reserve, Rajasthan. Forest Department, Government of Rajasthan.

Silvertown, J. (2009). A new dawn for citizen science. Trend Ecol. Evol. 24, 467–471. doi: 10.1016/j.tree.2009.03.017

Simpson, N., Steward, K., Schroeder, C., Cox, M., Huebner, K., & Wasley, T. (2016). Overpasses and underpasses: Effectiveness of crossing structures for migratory ungulates. The Journal of Wildlife Management, 80(8), 1370-1378.

The Local. Wildlife road collisions hit record high in Sweden. Posted Jan. 5, 2018. https://www.thelocal.se/20180105/wildlife-road-collisions-hit-record-high-in-sweden

United States Department of Transportation and the Federal Highway Administration. Wildlife-Vehicle Collision Reduction Study. August 2008. https://www.fhwa.dot.gov/publications/research/safety/08034/08034.pdf

Union of Concerned Scientists 2015 CO2 Emissions Data by Country Report https://www.ucsusa.org/global-warming/science-and-impacts/science/each-countrys-share-of-co2.html#.W6wECpNKhQJ

Volker, John 2014 1.2 Billion Vehicles On World's Roads Now, 2 Billion By 2035: Report. https://www.greencarreports.com/news/1093560_1-2-billion-vehicles-on-worlds-roads-now-2-billion-by-2035-report.

Waetjen, D.P, Schilling, F. August 2017 Frontiers in Ecology and Evolution, https://doi.org/10.3389/fevo.2017.00089. Road Ecology Center, Department of Environmental Science and Policy, University of California, Davis, Davis, CA, United States

REWILDING
INITIATIVES

*The Elk Refuge in the Greater Yellowstone Ecosystem teems with
wildlife, as would much more of North America if adequately
protected; though, sadly, Bison are still persecuted when they leave
nearby Yellowstone National Park, due to livestock interests.*
© Darren Burkey

MOGOLLON WILDWAY RAMBLE: FIELD NOTES FROM SCOUTING A PROPOSED NATIONAL SCENIC TRAIL

BY KELLY BURKE, GRAND CANYON WILDLANDS COUNCIL COFOUNDER AND WILD ARIZONA EXECUTIVE DIRECTOR; AND JOHN DAVIS, *REWILDING EARTH* EDITOR AND SCOUT

Mexican Wolves are trying to return to the Grand Canyon via the Mogollon Wildway. Lone, intrepid Lobos have made the journey toward home, setting down four swift paws along the forest pathways out from the heart of their recovery area in America's Southwest. Yet, deadly highway crossings and the arbitrary boundaries set by wildlife agencies remain serious obstacles to Nature's irrepressible rewilding.

Wildlife advocates aim to win El Lobo's freedom to roam and protect the broad regional wildlife corridor that sweeps west and north from the Gila Wilderness in southwest New Mexico to Grand Canyon National Park in northern Arizona. When explorers and naturalists from Wildlands Network (wildlandsnetwork.org) and The Rewilding Institute (rewilding.org) followed the likely routes and signs of wild Lobos during TrekWest in 2013 (a 5,000-mile exploration of a proposed Western Wildway along the Spine of

Male tarantulas, like the one John saw on Rim Road, are often moving in autumn, looking for females. © *Susan Morgan*

the Continent, from northern Sonora, Mexico, to southern British Columbia, Canada), they included the Mogollon Wildway in a summarizing 'Critical Wildways' paper. The Mogollon Wildway ranked among the top twenty priorities for the Intermountain West in that paper.

The Rewilding Institute, Grand Canyon Wildlands Council, Arizona Wilderness Coalition, Wildlands Network, New Mexico Wild, and kindred groups are now calling upon land stewards and users, diverse communities, and other decision-makers to work cooperatively to conserve and restore wild lands and waters connecting the Gila wildlands complex with the Grand Canyon wildlands complex and beyond. **One approach some of us propose to reconnect these wild lands and waters is establishing a new national scenic trail, the Lobo Trail.**

The trail would run the length of the scenic Mogollon Rim and into the heart of the Gila, linking the Arizona Trail to the Continental Divide Trail, while following short stretches of these trails at its far ends. The trail's purpose is to connect human hearts to the wildlife corridor, through the wild and increasingly popular experience of long distance foot travel, with possibilities for route finding in more rugged sections or through a simple ramble in beautiful wild country. We are also exploring the feasibility of delineating a companion bike-pack route, mostly following existing Forest Service and BLM roads.

Reasons to better protect and broaden this existing but tenuous habitat connection can be loosely put in five camps: land, wildlife, water, people, and climate.

Land

The Mogollon Wildway goes from the Gila backcountry's modest elevations clothed in sunny pine forests, to Arizona's tallest mountains, the oft snow-capped San Francisco Peaks, to our continent's deepest incision, Grand Canyon. The Mogollon

Wildway links the Gila wildlands complex with the Grand Canyon wildlands complex via the Mogollon Plateau and Rim. The Mogollon Rim comprises much of the southwestern edge of the vast and geologically superlative Colorado Plateau.

Wildlife

Thanks to heroic work from southwestern conservationists, the Gila backcountry is among the few places in the lower 48 states to have retained and regained its top carnivores. Against long odds, Fish & Wildlife Service released Mexican Wolves, Lobos, into the Gila wilds in the late 1980s. Despite persecution by some ranchers and gunners, Lobos have thrived in the Gila wildlands complex since then and have tried to expand their recovery. Pumas have survived centuries of persecution, and they continue to play their essential herbivore-regulating role in the forests and grasslands and riparian zones of the Gila watershed. Coyote, foxes, Bobcat, Badger, weasels, Ringtail, snakes, and raptors also continue to play crucial stabilizing roles. Rare species here include Gila Trout, Gila Chub, Loach Minnow, Southwestern Willow Flycatcher, Least Bells Vireo, Mexican Spotted Owl, and Mexican Wolf.

Lobos are attempting to disperse just as we would expect—and as we should welcome—northwest from their small official Recovery Area in the Gila and Apache National Forests of southwest New Mexico and southeast Arizona along the Mogollon Plateau and Rim toward the Grand Canyon. Several intrepid Lobo scouts have made the long journey, but they've been captured and returned to the small area where they are allowed. Politics, not biology, stands in the way of their recolonizing more of the Mogollon Wildway and regaining old strongholds across the Colorado Plateau.

Water

Springs are happily abundant but sadly degraded along the Mogollon Rim. They represent some of the "low hanging fruit" for future conservation efforts. The Springs Stewardship Institute (springstewardshipinstitute.org) is working throughout the Colorado Plateau and beyond with land-owners, land management agencies, tribes, and all who care about healthy waters and lands, to identify and conserve freshwater springs. Springs are hotbeds of biodiversity, providing habitat and/or sustenance to thousands of species, many of them endemic to a small number of springs.

Sadly, most springs in the US Southwest—and probably by now most worldwide, though few assessments have been done—have been damaged by livestock, logging, roads, mining, and other exploitive uses. Relatively simple measures can conserve the wildlife and water of springs, like fencing out livestock, creating no-cut buffers around them, and modifying culverts to afford natural water flow and aquatic wildlife movement.

The Mogollon Wildway is rich in springs—probably containing thousands, judging by Springs Stewardship Institute's preliminary surveys—and many of these springs have rare and imperiled species. In particular, the Mogollon Rim north of Route 260 is rife with springs, enhancing its appeal to hikers and cyclists as well as making it ecologically critical. A hiker or gravel-biker can get a good sense of the Mogollon Rim's profusion of springs by walking around the General Springs area, on either side of the Rim Road (FS road 300). Water runs in all directions, with freshets creating some of lushest meadows and forests one can find in Arizona. The springs from General Springs flowing south gather to form the East Verde River.

Streams, which are usually fed by springs, are equally critical ecologically and hydrologically; and again, the Mogollon Wildway is richly endowed. Arizona's two designated Wild & Scenic Rivers, the Verde River and its tributary Fossil Creek, both head on the

Mogollon Plateau, as do Oak, Sycamore, Wet Beaver, and West Clear Creeks. The Verde River forms a cottonwood-lined oasis in the high desert, popular with paddlers and vital to wide-ranging animals like Puma, Coyote, Ringtail, Javelina, deer, raptors, and songbirds, as well as to the fish and macro-invertebrates in its waters.

The White Mountains of Arizona, particularly Mt Baldy (11,400'), collect much of the region's moisture coming from the Gulf of Mexico or the Pacific Ocean and are thus a major water source for the Southwest. Here are the headwaters of the Little Colorado, Salt, and San Francisco Rivers.

Farther southeast in the Mogollon Wildway is the watershed of the Gila River, a main artery of the Southwest, ecologically and hydrologically. The Gila and its main tributaries in southwest New Mexico and southeast Arizona, the Blue, San Francisco, and Mimbres Rivers, are home to rare fish, and they have some of the healthiest riparian habitat in the West, thanks to remoteness, Wilderness Area designations, and partial removal of livestock from some sensitive habitats.

When assessments for potential Wolf recovery habitat were done years ago, the complex of small mountain ranges from the Blue Range Primitive Area through the Gila Wilderness ranked as outstanding, due to this being an exceptionally well-watered part of the Southwest, and hence rich in prey for carnivores. For anecdotal comparison, one of us (John D.) saw on a typical day of bike-packing through the Gila and Apache National Forests about fifteen Javelina (Collared Peccary), twenty Mule Deer, much sign of Elk (but they were hiding, as it was rifle season), and a Sonoran White-tail Deer—all potential food for Wolves and Pumas (and then for the scavengers who follow them).

Peoples

Like much of the Southwest, the Mogollon Wildway holds the homelands to many native tribes, all subjected to Euro-Americans displacing or killing them and restricting those who remained to small politically-defined areas. The Mogollon Plateau and Rim—which take their name from the Mogollon people, who long lived in this area—still have abundant cultural evidence and influence of the gatherer-hunter-grower tribes that preceded our agricultural-industrial civilization. Mimbres art, world famous now, originates from this area. Many museums, especially the Museum of Northern Arizona in Flagstaff, contain pottery, arrowheads, and other crafts from the peoples of this area; and visitors often find additional artifacts (and, if ethical, leave them in place).

Climate

In this century of climate chaos, habitat connections, especially altitudinal and latitudinal, become vital to the survival of sensitive and wide-ranging species. Running roughly southeast to northwest, and with elevations ranging from below 3,000 feet to more than 12,000 feet, the Mogollon Wildway—if we adequately protect it—will afford safe travel routes to cooler climes and relict micro-climates for species that otherwise might be doomed by anthropogenic global overheating.

Paths Therein

The National Forests and other public lands of Mogollon Wildway are already liberally sprinkled with trails and scarred with roads, but connecting them into a National Scenic Trail and a bike-pack route would require much scouting and map study, some of which has happened during the Grand Canyon Wolf Recovery Project's Paseo del Lobo outings (gcwolfrecovery.org) and some during TrekWest and follow-up trips. Basically, the Lobo Trail can use and connect a southern part of the Continental Divide Trail near Silver City with a northern part of the Arizona Trail to South Rim. Most of it between these two great thru-trails, too, can follow shorter existing trails, and for bike travel, lightly used roads.

Sights And Sounds Along The Mogollon Wildway

Collectively, in our explorations of the Mogollon Wildway, we have had countless wonderful experiences with wildlife, waterways, and weather. A few personal anecdotes help illustrate what a back-packer or bike-packer may experience here:

Mogollon Baldy, a high-point in the Gila Wilderness at 10,750 feet, and often snow-shrouded, shimmers in bright summer sun and swarming orange lady-bug beetles.

A stunningly beautiful Red-faced Warbler sings from atop a cottonwood tree in a riparian forest of the Mimbres River.

From the heart of America's first designated Wilderness Area, the Gila, howls a pack of Lobos, released in the area Aldo Leopold helped protect, after his Green Fire epiphany of a century ago, in which his watching the fierce green fire dying in the eyes of a Wolf he'd just shot made him realize the mountains want Wolves.

An American Dipper, or Water Ouzel as John Muir preferred to call this marvelous underwater-diving songbird, flies quickly from the rapids of the Middle Fork Gila River to her nest under a rock overhang above the water.

Gila Trout lurk in the shadows of the West Fork Gila, occasionally darting for flies that alight on the shining waters.

Trails in the heart of the Gila Wilderness, remote from human exploitation, are liberally strewn with scats of carnivores, including Bobcat, Puma, Gray Fox, Lobo, Black Bear, and weasels.

A big dark object moving through the pinyon-juniper woodland across the San Francisco River resolves itself into a foraging Black Bear.

Two hikers watch the sun set and full moon rise from atop Loco Peak. Walking back to their tents afterward, they are followed at a respectful distance by a curious Puma.

A whiptail scorpion big as a mouse walks ponderously down to the Blue River.

An extended family of ten Javelinas, including several darling little ones, scurries out of sight into the willows along Dry Blue Creek as they hear the bicycle approach on the dirt road above.

The deeply incised Black River flows steadfastly past that famed Green Fire site, decade after decade of serving the whole biota, from Wolves to warblers.

Lush meadows amid aspen stands, soon to be spangled in wildflowers, emerge slowly from melting spring snow on the flanks of Mt Escudilla, where roamed the last known Grizzly Bear in Arizona.

Coyotes answer either the full moon or the bugling Elk in the fall rut north of the Mogollon Rim, as a light freeze frosts the ground.

Into the grand old-growth Ponderosa Pines of McKenna Park disappears a herd of Elk. Nearby, a Bobcat flits in and out of the shadows cast by the great tree trunks.

In autumn, the San Francisco Peaks become grandly though distantly obvious, even from a hundred miles south across the vast Mogollon Plateau, when snow brightens their summits.

A black male tarantula walks boldly across the Rim Road as a bicyclist watches with awe, then hastens the spider's crossing, to ensure he not get hit by a passing vehicle.

A horned lizard, short and squat, suns itself on a sandstone slab, mid-way down the Mogollon Rim escarpment, not far above lush Tonto Creek, on a warm autumn day.

A young Badger, perhaps unacquainted with people, can't quite decide whether to run from a hiker or investigate this strange tall two-legged thing, but finally decides caution is the better part of valor and trundles away from the trail.

Elk heavily trot and Pronghorn lightly bound away from a lone hiker following the Arizona Trail across Anderson Mesa, toward Flagstaff.

Conclusion

Lobos, Pumas, Black Bears, weasels, raptors, trout, chubs, lizards, snakes, flowers, trees, back-packers, horse-packers, and bike-packers deserve safe ways to move between the two greatest wildlands complexes in the Southwest, the Gila and the Grand Canyon. The Mogollon Wildway is that link, and it is still relatively intact but faces many ongoing threats, including inappropriate, tax-payer subsidized livestock grazing and logging on public lands and housing sprawl on private lands. Increased public support is needed to keep the Mogollon Wildway safe for wildlife movement and habitation. A National Scenic Trail and companion bike-pack route can help raise the profile of this little-known yet gorgeous area and generate momentum for its greater conservation. We'll know we've done our job well here when anywhere along the Lobo Trail, after a long day of admiring wildflowers and songbirds and Puma scrapes, we can fall asleep in our tents to the musical howls of nearby Wolf families.

FOLLOWING ALICE THE MOOSE: NOTES FROM AN A2A RECONNAISSANCE HIKE

BY JOHN DAVIS, *REWILDING EARTH* EDITOR AND SCOUT

Were I a Moose, I'd be breaking all the rules. I'm climbing mountains merely for views of this glorious watery wooded landscape, cursing at thick bushwhacks through spruce/fir forest that a Moose might forage in winter; aiming my Hornbeck solo canoe for clear open water, rather than wading and feeding in the nearby swamps and marshes; carrying too much weight in my Osprey backpack; and gingerly side-stepping the muddy trail sections Moose walk right through. Still, a week into our A2A Reconnaissance Hike, I've seen a good bit of what Alice the Moose saw when she journeyed fifteen years ago from the middle of New York's huge Adirondack Park to Ontario's fabled Algonquin Park.

When Alice made this long trek, she inadvertently confirmed the Algonquin to Adirondack (or Adirondack to Algonquin— either way, A2A) habitat linkage (wildlife corridor, or *wildway*, as some of us prefer to say) that biologists had identified. She inspired a conservation effort that has grown into the A2A Collaborative (A2Acollaborative.org), of which The Rewilding Institute is a participant. A2A partners on both sides of the border spent much of a month exploring A2A on the ground in autumn 2017, simultaneously hiking northwest and southeast from our respective parks toward the Thousand Islands in the Saint

*Moose, both male and female, may disperse long distances in search
of mates or better forage. Unfortunately, in southern parts of their
range, Moose may be harmed by global overheating.*
© *Roderick MacIver Arts*

Lawrence River, to celebrate Alice the Moose and the wildway she revealed and to investigate the possibility of an eventual A2A International Scenic Trail. I was lucky enough to do much of the hiking and paddling and bicycling on the US side; and my scouting confirmed the wildness of this region and its great appeal for outdoorspeople, as well as wildlife.

Trails For Wildways

The Rewilding Institute (rewilding.org) works with Wildlands Network (wildlandsnetwork.org), regional conservation groups, and land trusts to protect wildways—wide wild habitat connections—at all scales, from local to continental. Sometimes, we scout or promote footpaths as means of engendering wildways protection (as the Appalachian Trail has inspired land conservation along its length). In particular, we've been exploring and advocating trails with Champlain Area Trails (champlainareatrails.org) for further protection of Split Rock Wildway; with Wildlands Network and Southwest wildlands groups to build support for Mogollon Wildway; and with the Algonquin to Adirondack Collaborative (A2A) to create a regional identity for the wildway linking these two great parks. Here we share notes from the US part of an A2A Reconnaissance Hike in late 2017, which will help guide our exploration and advocacy work for 2019 and beyond.

Globally Important Connection

A2A has long been recognized as a regional habitat connection priority, though it has not yet been fully enough appreciated as a habitat link of continental and global importance. Yet, a careful look at geologic and geographic and human footprint maps of eastern North America shows this to be among the most promising links between wildlands in the United States and wildlands in Canada. Indeed, eastern North American lands can be roughly divided between areas south of the Great Lakes and their outlet, the St. Lawrence River, and areas north. There are not many easy crossings for terrestrial animals of this vast waterway system (one of Earth's great drainages). The A2A area, which geologists know as the Frontenac Axis or Arch, essentially an arm of the Canadian Shield reaching southeast to and through Adirondack Park, offers a relatively safe crossing of the St Lawrence through the Thousand Islands, as well as sparsely peopled, still mostly forested habitat connecting the two great parks.

Probably many other wide-ranging animals before and after Alice have used the A2A wildlife connection; and it becomes even more important in a warming climate. Likely the famous young male Puma, posthumously dubbed Walker, who journeyed from South Dakota's Black Hills to Adirondack Park before being killed—still looking for a mate—by a car in Connecticut in 2011 (see Will Stolzenburg's powerful book *Heart of a Lion*) came south from Ontario via A2A. If Wolves are to recolonize the northeastern US, likely they will disperse southeast from Algonquin Park via the A2A connection—though many guns and traps around the Park and roads near the border stand in their way.

Ambling A2A

For my little part of the A2A exploration, I began on a picture-perfect fall-foliage day, October 1st, on the Adirondack Interpretive Center trails outside Newcomb, with my friends Richard Grover (A2A co-founder and visionary), Tom Butler (author of *Wildlands Philanthropy* and other conservation books), and Bart Howe (intrepid explorer and mountaineer). Aptly, we camped the first night on Moose Pond, nestled beneath the western High Peaks. My friends had to return to their jobs next day, and I figured I could hike the rest of the circuit way around Moose Pond and to the Cold River and then along Long Lake in a day (due in Long Lake to talk with an *Adirondack Explorer* writer late October 3rd), so I left the trail and followed streams up to a starkly open clear slide cutting down the west side of Santanoni. This I scaled hurriedly, not at all as a Moose would, to get fabulous views of the lake-studded country westward, which Alice had traversed and I'd soon hike and paddle across. Above the slide, spruce/fir forest got thick; and I was not appreciating the Moose browse I thrashed through, before finally gaining the Santanoni summit (4,600+'). Then I followed "herd paths" (ADK peak-baggers' term for the muddy unmarked trails up some of the more remote High Peaks) to summits of Panther (highest of multiple Adirondack mountains named "Panther"—would that we still had as many of the great cats themselves!) and Couchsachraga.

North of Moose Pond, the hiking and equestrian trail becomes less well-maintained but still lovely. Fittingly, I saw Moose tracks following the trail in several places. It took me to Cold River, near the farthest place from a road you can get in Adirondack Park and one of the farthest places from a road you can get in the eastern United States—only about five miles, not nearly so remote as a wildlands explorer, four- or two-legged, would prefer. Then I was on Adirondack Park's famous Northville-Placid Trail—part of which would be good to include in a larger A2A trail—as far as the village of Long Lake.

After interviews in Long Lake, there followed three days of classic Adirondack waterway travel, paddling across lakes and along meandering streams, and walking the portage trails (all easily passable but some muddy) between them. This is also great Moose country, and I saw their tracks often, as well as sign of bear, otter, and other wide-ranging mammals, plus eagles, hawks, Osprey, kingfishers, ducks, and geese in flight. One bold Bald Eagle chased a full-grown Canada Goose past the end of Little Tupper Lake and out of sight. Particularly Moosy and mossy sections include the slow winding sedge- and alder-lined stream between Little Tupper Lake and Rock Pond, and Shingle Shanty and Harrington Brooks flowing into Lake Lila. Likewise, the Oswegatchie River, draining the heart of the proposed Bob Marshall wildlands complex, meanders through boreal habitats.

Indeed, as I made this watery traverse, I recalled that much of the job of securing A2A within Adirondack Park itself is completing protection of the Bob Marshall (or Oswegatchie) wildlands complex, in the northwest quadrant of the Park, as outlined in the past by Adirondack Council (adirondackcouncil. org) and other Adirondack conservation groups. I traversed this many years ago southwest to northeast, but my traverse this time, southeast to northwest, seemed even more beautiful a journey.

I'll close for now with my closest Moose encounter, perhaps my nearest approach to the spirit of Alice. At dusk of my fifth trekking day, I'd sat mesmerized by Big Deer Pond, between Lows Lake and the Oswegatchie River, watching Beavers and a Muskrat foraging peaceably near each other, hearing Coyotes howling in the distance, and admiring ducks alighting gracefully on the still water. When I could no longer see the animals, I retired to my tent, to study maps and write notes. Just as I was about to turn out my solar lamp and collapse in a hiker's deep weary sleep, a terrific crashing sounded not a hundred yards from my camp. My lamp was not strong enough to catch the creature, but by the noise of him or her moving through the trees, and by the tracks on the portage path next day, I know the big beast was a Moose—moving west, leading me the safest way toward Algonquin Park.

FACING THE CHALLENGES OF DAM REMOVAL IN ALASKA

BY BRAD MEIKLEJOHN, THE CONSERVATION FUND

The Conservation Fund has nearly completed the demolition of the long-abandoned Lower Eklutna River dam, near the Native Village of Eklutna, Alaska. The Lower Eklutna River Dam Removal Project is the most ambitious river restoration project ever attempted in Alaska.

Death To Deadbeat Dams - By The Numbers

In the United States there are roughly 26,000 dams that are considered to be at high risk of failure, and many of these are abandoned or "deadbeat" dams that no longer serve any useful purpose. The push to take down these obsolete dams has gained momentum as 1,275 dams have been dismantled in the past 30 years. According to the non-profit American Rivers, a record high number of 87 dams were removed in 2017. Some of the largest high-profile dam removals have been completed in recent years on the Elwha and White Salmon rivers in Washington and the Kennebec and Penobscot rivers in Maine. Four major dams slated for removal in the near future are on Oregon's Klamath River. Real progress has yet to be made in dismantling the motherlode of deadbeat dams found on the Snake River in Washington and Idaho.

The Conservation Fund has nearly completed the demolition of the long-abandoned Lower Eklutna River dam, near the Native Village of Eklutna, Alaska. The Lower Eklutna River Dam Removal Project is the most ambitious river restoration project ever attempted in Alaska.
© Brad Meiklejohn

The Lower Eklutna River dam was built in 1928 as part of Alaska's first hydroelectric project. Located in a dramatic 400-foot deep canyon, access to the dam site was a severe challenge during the construction (and demolition) of the dam. In construction, a tram cart delivered concrete down the cliff face to the workers below. This hardy crew worked throughout an entire Alaskan winter to complete the dam in a year's time.

The dam itself was a concrete arch whose dimensions were 70 feet wide, 100 feet tall, and 9 feet thick at the dam base. This structure pooled and diverted water through a half-mile tunnel to a generating station nearby. Power ran by wire twenty miles south to Anchorage, providing the first reliable supply of electricity to this frontier settlement. The Lower Eklutna power project operated until the early 1950s when it was decommissioned and ultimately abandoned. Ownership of the dam remained in limbo until the Alaska Native Claims Settlement Act conveyed the dam and all the surrounding land to the Eklutna Village Native Corporation.

The Eklutna River was once a prolific salmon-producing river that supported the Eklutna Dena'ina people, who located their village on Cook Inlet's Knik Arm near the mouth of the Eklutna River. Although the Native Eklutna people are still there, the salmon are greatly diminished, due to a succession of water diversions and hydropower projects which cut off water flow and fish passage in the Eklutna River. Repeated studies over several decades have recommended the removal of the Lower Eklutna River dam as an essential first step in restoring the Eklutna River.

Despite being decommissioned in the 1950s, the Lower Eklutna dam survived the 1964 Alaska Earthquake (magnitude 8.2) with no signs of impairment. Though the dam remained structurally sound and showed no imminent signs of failure, the State of Alaska Office of Dam Safety had long-recommended its orderly removal. Because the structure was an orphaned, unmaintained dam upstream of three bridges, a major highway, and a railroad, there was significant public safety benefit to removing the dam in a controlled manner rather than waiting for its ultimate failure.

Removing the Lower Eklutna River dam is the first step in a multi-phase restoration plan for the Eklutna River. The principal conservation outcomes that will result from removing the Lower Eklutna River dam are:

- Restore fish passage to a seven-mile reach of the Eklutna River.
- Improve spawning habitat in the lower Eklutna River for five species of salmon and Dolly Varden.
- Reestablish natural river functions in the lower Eklutna River.
- Reestablish habitat connectivity for fish and other wildlife on the Lower Eklutna River.
- Take a major step toward the recovery of the entire Eklutna River watershed.

Although removal had been discussed for decades, The Conservation Fund began to actively pursue the dam removal in 2014. After identifying key partners, in collaboration with Eklutna Inc. (the Eklutna Native village corporation and landowner) and HDR (primary technical consultants for the project), the Fund initiated project scoping, baseline research, and assessment of construction methodologies in 2015. With necessary permits secured in 2016, site preparation was completed in fall of 2016. The 2017 work season saw the removal of 90% of the dam structure, the remainder of which should be entirely removed this spring. Site remediation and negotiations for the restoration of in-stream flows and monitoring of spawning, turbidity, and sediment transport will continue into 2020 and beyond.

Funding for the $7.5 million project was provided largely by The Conservation Fund, with additional financial support from the Rasmuson Foundation, the M.J Murdock Charitable Trust, the National Fish and Wildlife Foundation, the Open Rivers Fund of the Hewlett Foundation, Resources Legacy Fund, the Marnell

Corporation, the Alaska Sustainable Salmon Fund, Patagonia, Orvis, Wells Fargo, and the Alaska Community Foundation.

While most major dam removals take decades to complete, this project has gone from concept to near-completion in only three years. The rapid advancement of the project is due in large part to the fact that most of the money came from private sources, short circuiting the lengthy delays that inevitably come with government funding. With a backlog of thousands of deadbeat dams that are slated for removal across the nation, this project serves as a model of efficiency and cost-effectiveness.

In addition to the funding challenges, there were severe technical challenges to the project. The Lower Eklutna River dam is located in a 400-foot deep canyon with sheer walls and no road access. Accessing the dam involved the installation of the state's largest crane with a 400-foot reach and construction of a dramatic 500-step aluminum staircase into the canyon. An additional complication was working on and around the 70-feet deep accumulation of 300,000 cubic yards of silt, sand, and gravel that had built up behind the dam following its abandonment in 1955. Combined with the tight confines of the canyon, these unstable and dynamic sediments required caution and creativity.

Concerns for the downstream infrastructure ruled out blasting the dam. Instead, a combination of fracturing with expansive grout and hammering with pneumatic jackhammers was used to break the dam down into bite-sized chunks. Sediment management techniques included 10-foot by 20-foot polycarbonate "tundra mats" to keep the machinery out of the LaBrea-tar-like muck and a hydraulic mining monitor to move the sediment away from the work area.

Removing the Lower Eklutna River dam has already provided significant economic benefits by creating more than 30 jobs in construction, research, and project management for Native Alaskans through the partnership with the Native Village of Eklutna and the Eklutna Native Corporation. Additional benefits to all Alaskans include the recovery of Cook Inlet King Salmon and the potential restoration of a major Sockeye Salmon run just 30 minutes from Anchorage. Restored salmon runs will also help the endangered Beluga Whale with additional forage fish sources.

Although removal of the Lower Eklutna River dam will not by itself rebuild salmon runs to their historic levels, the mere presence of the dam has thwarted any other restoration efforts. The main limiting factor for salmon in the Eklutna River is very low water due to hydropower diversions. The Eklutna Power Project, a federal project further up the watershed from the Lower Eklutna dam, diverts 90% of the water out of the Eklutna watershed into a tunnel that services a powerhouse located on the Knik River. The power producers, a consortium of three utilities, have long argued that releasing water into the Eklutna River is pointless as long as the lower dam remains in place.

Complete recovery of the Eklutna River will depend on the restoration of water flows back into the Eklutna River. The Eklutna Power Project is authorized under the 1991 Eklutna-Snettisham Agreement, which requires the Eklutna Power Project operators to initiate mitigation for their impacts to fish and other wildlife no later than 2022. The state and federal regulatory agencies that have jurisdiction over the Eklutna Power project have taken the view that sufficient water flows must be restored to the Eklutna River to mitigate for 88 years of water diversions. Taking all the water out of a salmon-bearing river is no longer an acceptable practice.

Beyond the significant conservation benefits that will result from removing the Lower Eklutna River dam, this project has greater symbolism. One reason Alaska still has abundant salmon is because we have mostly avoided the mistake of building dams on salmon-bearing rivers. At the Eklutna River, Alaskans are recognizing the problems created by an ill-considered dam and are collaborating to fix those problems. We hope this project will be a constant reminder to Alaskans and other Americans that salmon and dams are generally incompatible.

RESCUING AN ENDANGERED CACTUS: RESTORING THE SANTA FE CHOLLA

BY NANCY LEHRHAUPT, CACTUS RESCUE PROJECT

Fifteen years ago two Santa Fe, New Mexico, residents decided to save an endangered local cactus called the Santa Fe Cholla *(Cylindropuntia viridiflora).* It grew in only a few areas close to Santa Fe and was being threatened by human encroachment and development. Their qualifications for this? Well, John "Obie" Oberhausen is a massage therapist, and Joe Newman is an industrial designer; but they had a passion for this vulnerable plant and the drive and will to want to change its fate.

Joe and Obie started collecting cuttings from the neglected and dying Santa Fe Cholla colony in downtown Santa Fe and propagating them in their yards. They even took apart packrat nests made out of cholla pieces to use as starts for new plants. They spoke to local nurseries, set up informational booths, lectured at local plant society gatherings, and gave away plants, all in an effort to make the plight of this endangered cactus known.

When people would ask them what conservation group they were with, they had no answer except to say they were just two guys trying to make a difference. As they generated more and more interest and excitement about their work, they decided to call themselves the Cactus Rescue Project. They now

The Santa Fe Cholla (Cylindropuntia viridiflora), *smaller and bushier than the common tree cholla with blooms of bronze or salmon, is now dotting gardens around Santa Fe and the Southwest.*
© *Susan Morgan*

have a website (cactusrescueproject.info) and a Facebook page (CactusRescueProject) and have expanded their efforts to include the promotion of all cactus as a xeric alternative for gardening in drought afflicted areas of the southwestern United States.

To this end, the Cactus Rescue Project (CRP) has put in free demonstration gardens all over Santa Fe and in the community in which they live, Eldorado. The garden at the Eldorado Community Center is one of the largest public cactus gardens in New Mexico. They have installed cactus gardens at a shopping center, school, senior center, wildlife center, government agency, and have adopted and planted a median. CRP now has 5 regular members (Obie, Joe, this author, Kris Palek, and Phillip Musser) and has garnered 75-100 community volunteers to help with projects and weeding parties. Every year, they give educational talks about cactus and the Santa Fe Cholla and once a year have an annual "cactus give-away," where they give away thousands of cactus cuttings pruned from their demonstration gardens.

"We started years ago with a few bins of 3-4 inch pieces of Santa Fe Cholla and now we have pickup trucks overflowing with 12 inch pieces for people to take home and plant," says Obie.

The community and volunteer interest in cactus was fantastic, but CRP efforts to save the Santa Fe Cholla had to go beyond planting them in a few gardens and promoting their use in private gardening. In order to truly save the cactus, they needed to reestablish them in nature.

About 5 years ago, Joe and Obie met the New Mexico State Botanist, Daniela Roth, who is responsible for the state's endangered plants. They decided to work together to save this cactus and a year later planted 400 Santa Fe Cholla starts on a local preserve in an attempt to start a new natural colony. The plants were GPS marked and documented so the State could monitor them annually to check on their survival. The project drew community volunteers who helped with preparation and planting. It was such a success that another 3 colonies were planted at sites around the city of Santa Fe in the following year and a half, and more are scheduled for this coming spring. One of this year's colony planting projects will include volunteer students from a local high school, Santa Fe Preparatory School, who are using it as a science experience.

Daniela Roth, whose support and involvement has been invaluable to the CRP effort, was quoted as saying, "Well, this is rapidly becoming the most ambitious conservation project in the state of New Mexico! Better yet, it's all based on volunteer effort! Congratulations! If all endangered plant projects would receive such enthusiastic input from the community, we would not have any endangered plants, and I could just focus on research."

Obie and Joe are not done with their plans for the Santa Fe Cholla. This spring they are working with the New Mexico Department of Transportation to plant cactus along a highway interchange as well as working with the Santa Fe Water Conservation Office on additional projects.

Joe and Obie know that though they may have been the impetus for this effort, it takes a community to make recovery happen. They are grateful to all the volunteers, local organizations, and responsive government officials who have helped make a difference to save an endangered plant, the beautiful and prickly Santa Fe Cholla.

PUMA RECOVERY FOR EASTERN WILDWAYS: A CALL TO ACTION

BY CHRIS SPATZ AND JOHN LAUNDRE, COUGAR REWILDING FOUNDATION

The history of humans and carnivores in North America since European colonization is lopsided and biocidal. Whereas attacks by native carnivores on humans are so rare as to be statistically insignificant, European settlers and their descendants have shot, trapped, and poisoned predators by the millions, declaring war especially on pumas and wolves. Within an historical blink of an eye, these carnivores were all but eliminated from the eastern two-thirds of the continent south of the boreal forest.

Now, in 2018, as we enter a century of climate chaos, only tiny eastern populations persist of the keystone predators who protect forests from over-browsing. A small remnant population of pumas (panthers) exists in south Florida, and a tiny reintroduced population of red wolves struggles for survival in coastal North Carolina. An unknown number of coyote/wolf hybrids wander the Northeast, but these opportunistic "coy-wolves" can easily enough scavenge deer and other animals shot or killed by cars that they are not reliable year-round hunters of the East's most over-abundant browser. The southern-most reproducing wolf population in eastern Canada is faring relatively well in Algonquin Park, but these wolves rarely escape guns, traps, and cars for long, if they leave the Park.

*Cousins to Cheetahs, Pumas are among the world's greatest athletes
and critical apex carnivores in many ecosystems across the Americas;
yet thus far, state and federal wildlife agencies are refusing to
consider reintroducing them to the US East.*
© Larry Master, masterimages.org

The national, government-sanctioned elimination of an entire trophic level was fueled by fears and myths brought over from Europe. We now know these fears and myths are unfounded, yet still they persist. Large carnivores are now recognized by science and art for the valuable role they play in ecosystem dynamics, being vital community members keeping herbivores in balance with vegetation and adding beauty and drama to life. Unfortunately, this knowledge came too late for the East where the niche of ungulate eater is largely vacant. The loss of predators has harmful consequences, including diminished populations of songbirds, salamanders, and wildflowers; hardwood saplings being eaten before they can mature; outbreaks of Lyme and other zoonotic diseases; and over a million (too-oft fatal) car/deer collisions across the country every year.

As eastern ecosystems continue to suffer from their loss of top predators, we are overdue to bring them back, to welcome home pumas and wolves. To that end, The Rewilding Institute (rewilding.org), Cougar Rewilding Foundation (cougarrewilding. org), Wildlands Network (wildlandsnetwork.org), and allied groups call upon our fellow conservationists and recreationists to work toward restoring healthy populations of all native species, but particularly top carnivores and other keystone members of our biota, across their native ranges. All species eliminated from their original ranges in North America deserve to be restored, if it's not too late (as it is for the passenger pigeon, Carolina parakeet, great auk, imperial woodpecker, sea mink, and others persecuted unto extinction).

Of highest priority, however, is restoring the puma, also known as cougar, panther, painter, catamount, and mountain lion (*Puma concolor*). Wolves are equally important, but their recovery in the East may be more complicated, for social and genetic reasons. Large canids seem to be regaining a claw-hold on their own, through wolves occasionally interbreeding with coyotes, who are so resourceful they are now thriving in most of the country (though perhaps taking on wolf characteristics so far mainly in the northeastern US and southeastern Canada; and again, not often playing the critical role of regulating deer herds).

We'll also not address in this paper the many other carnivores still playing—or having recently returned to play—vital roles in eastern ecosystems, except to note that conservationists should not be complacent about the long-term well-being of black bear, river otter, fisher, marten, weasels, bobcat, and foxes (whereas raccoons look poised to inherit the world, if humans eliminate most other sizable mammals!). Combinations of habitat fragmentation, climate chaos, and direct killing could leave any or all of these other carnivores in trouble eventually. We do want to quickly emphasize that although they may not generally be considered keystone species or apex predators, Canada lynx and wolverine are both vital members of boreal ecosystems in North America, and they richly deserve our conservation concern. Indeed, some conservationists have suggested that the lynx could be something of a "gateway cat" for preparing people in the US Northeast for puma recovery. Most of these carnivores are capable of wide dispersals, and most of them will need safe wildlife corridors between core habitats if they are to thrive in the coming, climatically-unstable, centuries.

Parlous Status

Once widespread across eastern North America, pumas now only survive in a small isolated population in south Florida, where they are protected as the Florida panther under the Endangered Species Act, but they are essentially walled into the southern part of the state by the Caloosahatchie channel and development alongside. Floridians are proud of their panthers, and direct persecution is no longer the problem. Habitat isolation and roads and cars are the main threats to their survival. In bad years, twenty or more of the elusive cats are killed on Florida's busy roads—

this despite Florida's exemplary efforts to install safe wildlife crossings on major roads. The wildlife crossings are still too few and far between, and many roads still completely lack them.

Meanwhile, across the rest of the East, the US Fish and Wildlife Service (FWS) has declared the "Eastern cougar" extinct. This is a doubly unfortunate decision. First, it is biologically unsound, as the latest taxonomic information suggests that all native North American pumas are of one subspecies; the other five subspecies being Central and South American. So in effect the FWS posited a fictional subspecies then declared it extinct, so as not to have to address the need for puma recovery in the East.

Second, FWS's declaration of extinction for the "Eastern cougar" may make recovering the great cat in the East more difficult, though paradoxically, it may open the door for a progressive state to reintroduce Pumas unilaterally. Rather than using the Endangered Species Act as a tool to protect and restore biodiversity, FWS seems to be using it as a tool to discourage restoration. Fish & Wildlife officials should instead acknowledge the ecological importance of pumas, West and East, and strive to restore viable populations of the big cat wherever ample cover and prey remain. Doing so would be consistent with the intent of the Endangered Species Act, even if the puma as a whole species is in no near-term danger of extinction. Regional extinction of the keystone predator is causing untold ecological losses, which FWS ignores to its discredit.

A pressing need for the Florida panther is to expand its ESA Critical Habitat, to expand its recovery range northward to wildlands in north Florida, Georgia, and beyond. Ample habitat and prey remain in the Florida Panhandle, the Ocala to Osceola to Okefenokee (O2O) connection, South Carolina's Cape Fear Arch and ACE Basin, North Carolina's Albemarle Peninsula, and in other relatively undeveloped parts of the Southeast Coastal Plain. Connections through the Piedmont are more dubious, so habitat restoration as well as safe wildlife crossings will be needed in the

Carolinas' foothills. Once in the Appalachians, Pumas should be able to spread north and south along the mountain range, if fully protected under the ESA. So far, federal and state wildlife officials have lacked the courage to reintroduce panthers farther north in their original range, except for an experimental release of sterile pumas from Texas in southern Georgia many years ago—which showed the big cats could thrive. However, though potential reintroduction sites were identified, and public attitude surveys showed strong support for them, reintroductions mandated in each iteration of the panther recovery plan have never been implemented.

Wild Wanderers

With little hope of pumas reestablishing from within the East, many conservationists turn to the West. Pumas have been trying to recolonize areas eastward from their strongholds in the Rockies, but thus far roads and guns are preventing gains beyond the Great Plains. There are five known small satellite populations east of the main front of puma occupancy: in the Cypress Hills of southern Saskatchewan; Missouri River corridor of eastern Montana; Badlands of North Dakota; Black Hills of South Dakota; and the Pine Ridge, Wildcat Hills, and Niobrara River Valley areas of Nebraska. For a time, it appeared these revived populations might serve as stepping-stones for eastward colonization. Recently, however, it has become clear that persecution rates are too high for these populations to expand. South Dakota, especially, has sanctioned the annual killing of dozens of pumas—including females—quelling hopes the Black Hills cats might spread east into the forests of the Great Lakes states.

Occasionally, almost miraculously, brave individual carnivores cover hundreds of miles—under cover of darkness, crossing busy roads and sneaking past guns sufficient to arm militias—and make it back to the northern Midwest or in even rarer cases to the Appalachians or Adirondacks. With pumas especially, these long-dispersers are usually young males, for young female pumas instinctively stay near their mothers' home ranges, whereas young males instinctively try to find territories farther away from their natal homes. (With wolves, females may disperse nearly as often and as far as males, and pairs sometimes disperse together, so distant recolonizations are more likely than with cougars.)

Essential to these long-distance movements are adequate dispersal corridors, and they still exist, tenuously. An Atlantic/Appalachian Wildway from the Southeast Coastal Plain through the Appalachians and Adirondacks to the Canadian Maritimes is achievable in our lifetimes (see *Rewilding North America* by Dave Foreman and *Big, Wild, and Connected* by John Davis)—if conservationists can successfully collaborate with conservation-minded land-owners and land, wildlife, and transportation agencies. Much of the Eastern Forest is still permeable to movement of wide-ranging species. A Great Lakes Wildway linking the Northern Forest from Minnesota and Ontario's Boundary Waters to the Gulf of St. Lawrence is also achievable, as is a Gulf Coast Wildway from east Texas through Florida's Panhandle. Other west-east connections, especially along major rivers, are likewise top ecological priorities (see John Laundre's book *Phantoms of the Prairie* for discussion of how and why cougars often disperse along waterways).

Corridors Necessary But Not Sufficient

Almost inevitably, however, the tragic outcome of these wild wanderers' heroic journeys is the young male keeps moving, looking for a mate, until he is finally shot or hit by a car. Science writer Will Stolzenberg wrote a beautiful book, *Heart of a Lion*, about the amazing journey of a young male puma who was born in South Dakota's Black Hills, embarked eastward to find a new home and a mate, traversed the northern Midwest, wandered in winter through northern New York's wild but puma-deprived Adirondacks, and was finally hit and killed by a car in Connecticut in 2011.

More recently, a healthy young male puma was needlessly dispatched in Kentucky by wildlife officials. Perhaps even more amazingly, a female puma apparently made it as far east as central Tennessee in 2016, and (judging by wildlife camera photos) persisted there a good while. Reports suggested that a hunter shot but did not kill her with an arrow, turned in his arrow; and from the blood on that, genetic analysis suggested a Black Hills origin for this female cat, too. Numerous tragic endings demonstrate that although continental wildways and smaller wildlife corridors are needed if we are to restore and maintain our natural heritage, they are not enough. For successful restoration of carnivores, *co-existence will be as important as corridors*. Until wildlife agencies and land-owners support carnivore conservation, the predatory guardians of biotic communities will be restricted to present ranges and imperiled even in some of those. Unfortunately, support for carnivore conservation is spotty and in some areas has waned recently.

In general, conservationists and caring citizens have been aghast at—and caught unprepared by—a new backlash against predators in the rural United States. The misnamed "Wildlife Services," a killing program of the federal Agriculture Department, is shooting and trapping thousands of predators a year, mostly in the West, and usually at the behest of ranching or agribusiness interests. (See Project Coyote's website, projectcoyote.org, and film *Killing Games*.) State wildlife agencies have sided with ranchers and commercial hunters in pressuring the Fish & Wildlife Service to remove protections for the wolf in the Northern Rockies. Now, too, we are seeing a hate campaign aimed at ending the red wolf recovery program in the Southeast.

Such vitriolic opposition to carnivore recovery appears to combine the deep fear many people still feel for big toothy animals with a confused association in some rural people's minds of wildlife restoration and big bad government. Wolves, alas, have come to be seen as liberal Democrats, through no political fault of their own (but perhaps an unwise decision on the part of some environmentalists to cast their lot wholly with the Democratic Party—which, by and large, shares the Neo-Cons' indifference to wild Nature).

Meanwhile, however, coyotes continue to prosper, and now thrive across most of the country, West and East, despite being frequently shot or trapped in many areas. Benefitting from compensatory reproductive capacity, they remain relatively numerous (by carnivore standards) even where their mortality rates are high, but their natural hunting behavior and social structures are disrupted by the guns and traps they face. Moreover, as long as there is an open season on coyotes, wolf recovery is unlikely. Several of the heroic wide-wandering wolves of recent years have covered hundreds of miles in quests to find new home ranges, only to be gunned down in cases of supposed mistaken identity with coyotes. Project Coyote was among the first wildlife advocacy groups to realize that treating coyotes with dignity and respect, rather than as vermin, is essential not just because they are beautiful predators in their own right, but also because other predators will remain unsafe so long as the war on coyotes continues. A crucial step in wider carnivore recovery efforts, then, is gaining at least partial protection for coyotes in states with potential for reestablishment of wolf or puma populations.

Conservationists need to work to restore and protect local, regional, and continental wildways. At the same time, however, we must build the public pressure to force wildlife agencies to restore and conserve the full natural array of wildlife and habitats. "Bait and bullet" domination of wildlife management is maximizing game numbers to the detriment of natural communities.

In short, wildlife corridors—wildways—are essential to long-term persistence of pumas and other wide-ranging species. Also paramount, though, are welcoming attitudes to the full range of wildlife, including big toothy animals.

Active Reintroduction

With the sad realization that pumas are not likely to successfully spread far eastward from the Rockies or northward from south Florida anytime soon, the groups issuing this plea ask other conservationists, recreationists, and all who love wildlife to build support for active reintroduction of pumas in at least five big core wildland complexes in the near future. Habitat assessments and public outreach should precede the reintroductions, but they should not be excuses for perpetual delays.

Core wildland complexes that have ample food and cover for pumas to thrive include these:

- Osceola National Forest in northern Florida through Pinhook Swamp to Okefenokee National Wildlife Refuge in southern Georgia (O2O), and along wilder parts of the Southeast Coastal Plain;
- Great Smoky Mountains National Park and surrounding National Forests in western North Carolina and eastern Tennessee;
- Monongahela National Forest and Canaan National Wildlife Refuge in the High Alleghenies of West Virginia;
- Shenandoah National Park and National Forests along the Blue Ridge in Virginia and North Carolina;
- Adirondack Park in northern New York, with links to the Green Mountains, Tug Hill Plateau, Algonquin Park, and Catskills.

There are many other areas in the East with plenty of deer to eat and forest in which to seek cover. With public acceptance, pumas could recolonize much of the East; and we could coexist

197

with them happily. The paradox is, many people say they'd welcome cougars if they came back on their own, but do not support government programs to restore the great cats; yet the cats are not likely to be able to recolonize without help from wildlife agencies.

Steps To Puma Recovery In East

With this realization, we recommend the following steps toward puma and other carnivore recovery in the East. These are condensed in part from writings by Dave Foreman (The Rewilding Institute), Helen McGuiness (Klandagi), and Christine Bolgiano, as well as this paper's authors (Cougar Rewilding Foundation). We invite other groups and individuals to add to and work on this list. It takes a community to save a corridor; and restoring missing keystone species will take a much broader conservation community than we presently have.

1. Put the puma in the East back on the Endangered Species list, as a Distinct Population Segment, and designate recovery zones for it in the northern Midwest, northern Florida and southern Georgia, Great Smoky Mountains National Park, Shenandoah National Park, Monongahela National Forest, north-central Pennsylvania forests, Catskills, Adirondacks, Green and White Mountains, and Maine Woods.

2. Identify and protect wildways along the Southeast Coastal Plain; through the Piedmont; along the Appalachians; through the Adirondacks to Ontario's Algonquin Park (A2A); across Maine's North Woods and northward into Quebec and New Brunswick; from the Black Hills and Badlands eastward along rivers and around the Great Lakes and across the Northern Forest of southern Ontario and Quebec and adjacent states to the Atlantic Ocean; and along the Gulf Coast from

Texas to Florida, expanding northward to take in the Ozarks.

3. Create strong financial and social incentives for conservation on private lands, including property tax exemptions, payments for conservation easements, payments for ecosystem services, funds to restore broad riparian buffers, and a more ecologically-informed Wetland Reserve Program.

4. Expand and link existing protected areas on public lands, especially Wilderness Areas, National Parks, and National Wildlife Refuges.

5. Fully fund the Land and Water Conservation Fund. Create new Wilderness Areas and National Parks, including the proposed High Alleghenies National Park or Headwaters of the Nation National Monument in West Virginia, Maine Woods National Park in Maine, and Three Borders International Peace Park in New Brunswick, Quebec, and Maine.

6. Close unneeded back-roads on public lands, federal, and state, to create larger road-free cores and to reduce waste of tax-payer money.

7. Reform wildlife management at state and federal levels so that it conserves and restores the full range of native wildlife, rather than maximizing game numbers.

8. Broaden the base of wildlife funding to include excise taxes not just on hunting and fishing gear but also on other outdoor gear, and reinvest modest amounts of state sales taxes and tourist expenses associated with wildlife-watching for wildlife conservation.

9. Make at least one state (perhaps a relatively progressive one like Vermont) a model for democratic and biocentric wildlife conservation, and then spread that model to other states.

10. Bring to schools at all levels more natural history and education on the importance of keystone species, particularly apex carnivores; teach co-existence. Expand tracking programs to help people identify more with their wild neighbors and welcome returned wild neighbors.

11. Make our built environment, our transportation and communication networks particularly, more permeable to wildlife movement and durable in the face of climate chaos. Get safe wildlife crossings on major roads.

12. Build a coalition of support not only for enhancing possible natural recolonization efforts but also for active *reintroduction* efforts as needed.

13. Disband the federal predator-killing program, "Wildlife Services"; and replace it with a program that helps farmers and other land-owners co-exist with native predators, in part through depredation compensation programs and provision of guard dogs and llamas.

14. Conduct habitat assessments and social acceptance surveys in states where puma reintroduction may be feasible.

15. Reintroduce pumas to core wildland complexes in the East, including Okefenokee National Wildlife Refuge, Smoky Mountains and Shenandoah National Parks, Monongahela National Forest (or a bigger park comprised largely of NF lands), Adirondack Park, and Green and White Mountain National Forests.

Obviously, these steps go way beyond what any one group or even network of groups can accomplish. To restore and protect our countries' great natural heritage, East and West, will require cooperation from wildlife agencies, land-owners, hunters, fishers, hikers, skiers, bicyclists, climbers, birders... everyone who wishes to see the beauty and wildness of North America passed on intact to future generations. Carnivores test our generosity as a people.

If we are generous enough, our children may know the joy of hearing wolves howl on moonlit nights and finding fresh tracks in the sand of a mama puma and her cubs slipping quietly along a river-bank.

A NATIONAL CORRIDORS CAMPAIGN FOR RESTORING AMERICA THE BEAUTIFUL

BY MICHAEL E. SOULÉ

"Sentiment without action is the ruin of the soul."

—ED ABBEY

*C*ritics often state that the American Era is finished, that America can no longer claim to be a "shining city on a hill," a beacon for those seeking opportunity, adventure, or even seeking a compelling story to tell family and friends back home in New Jersey, France, or South Africa. Critics of America also proclaim the demise of the American dream. Such speculation is premature. We believe that hope still springs from the land in rural towns from Montana to New Mexico, from Utah to Colorado, from Oregon to Georgia. The concept of a National Corridors Campaign (NCC), proposed here for discussion, is an expression of American optimism.

Please note that the emphasis in this paper is on the Spine of the Continent (Western Wildway) corridor because it is the most iconic and least disturbed of the continental wildways, and it is where many conservation groups have begun networking in the last decade. A National Corridors Campaign, if successful, however, will protect connected wildlife habitats and

John Davis starts 40-Mile Chiricahuas hike. © *Kim Vacariu*

recreational greenways through the Southeast Coastal Plain and Appalachian Mountains (Eastern Wildway) and through the Pacific Coast Ranges and undeveloped shores (Pacific Wildway), and eventually also reconnect Nature and people through the Great Plains, along the Gulf Coast, around the Great Lakes, across the Boreal Forest, and in other realms, east-west as well as north-south, aquatic as well as terrestrial, where biodiversity restoration and wilderness recreation is still possible.

1. Background

The conservation movement in the US has succeeded in protecting much biodiversity in the last half-century. We've helped establish millions of acres of parks, wilderness areas, and wildlife refuges. Sadly, however, we've lost more ground than we've gained. On average, we lose 1.6 million acres of private land a year to development and fragmentation, and similarly large amounts of public land are degraded by industrial resource extraction and motorized off-road recreation. Even in the grandest part of the continent, the Rocky Mountains, nature reserves are too small and isolated, and unprotected areas face a growing list of threats, which include population growth and exurban sprawl on private lands; industrial recreation and energy extraction on public lands; and the ideology of infinite economic growth that fuels these harmful trends.

So, what would constitute conservation success in the US? Many conservation biologists would define success as *the protection of inter-connected lands and waters that provide sufficient habitat and security for vigorous and well-distributed populations of all native species and the restoration of ecological functions provided by them, including:*

- *seed and pollen dispersal*
- *dispersal of (mostly young) animals necessary to maintain both genetic and demographic vigor and*

- *seasonal migrations of animals, either via traditional routes or new, pioneer routes necessitated by habitat disruption and climate change*
- *natural control of both (1) mesopredators such as house cats, raccoons, skunks, and some corvid birds and (2) the population sizes of some ungulates such as deer, elk, and moose*
- *maintenance of habitat diversity by grazing and browsing herbivores such as bison, prairie dogs, and beaver*
- *the capacity of species to shift their geographic distributions when and where necessitated by climate change.*

2. Launching A National Conservation And Recreation Corridors Campaign

Dozens of conservation organizations champion the restoration and protection of landscape permeability. These organizations are already engaged in multiyear campaigns to conserve connectivity along the Spine of the Continent and beyond. In the West, these regional initiatives include the construction of fencing and safe passage structures for wildlife across highways; implementation of connectivity-based national monuments in the Grand Canyon region; creation of a Northern Jaguar Reserve (northernjaguarproject.org) in the Sonoran Desert Wildway; and formation of a Western Landowner's Alliance (westernlandowners.org).

In the East, the initiatives include *Staying Connected* in the Northern Appalachians (stayingconnectedinitiative.org), which partnership seeks to increase conservation in eight critical linkages in the US and Canada; collaboration with the *Vermont Agency of Transportation* to reduce the effects of roads on wildlife; and strategic acquisitions by land trusts like the Northeast Wilderness Trust (newildernesstrust.org) in local wildways. In the Southeast Coastal Plain, the Wildlands Network (wildlandsnetwork.org) is leading the development of a regional conservation plan to connect and expand existing nature reserves in this hotspot of North American biodiversity.

The Rocky Mountains, running south-north through much of western North America, and including big parts of Mexico, the United States, and Canada, are where a national and international conservation corridor can most quickly be achieved. Some of the green infrastructure of such a continental corridor is in place, and mapping is ongoing to establish the route. The work has gained momentum since completion of TrekWest in 2013 (subject of the film *Born to Rewild*), and since publication of two eloquent books on conservation in the Rockies: Mary Ellen Hannibal's *The Spine of the Continent* and Cristina Eisenberg's *The Carnivore Way*.

3. Adapting To The New (Political/ Economic) Normal

A basic goal of a national conservation and recreation corridors campaign is connectivity—for wildlife, for human-powered recreation, and for ecological resilience in the face of change. *Such an outcome is only achievable by welcoming a wide range of partners to the corridors team, including partners with goals that benefit diverse social, economic, and environmental interests.*

We live in an era when fewer and fewer people venture outdoors and a diminishing percentage love nature for its own sake. Kids, especially, spend much more time on computers and television than they do exploring nearby woods and streams— in part because the nearby woods and streams have been paved over. The natural world is receding farther and farther from where people live and work.

An analysis of charitable giving in the US shows a shocking absence of caring about the outdoors. The preferred beneficiaries of charity today are religious institutions (about 45% of donations). Next come public health and cultural institutions. Less than one percent goes to nature and wildlife! This means that any campaign must appeal to a mainstream audience with diverse concerns.

Marketers and conservationists agree that any campaign must inspire hope. In the current economy, "hope" must include jobs and recreation. Though many of us love wildlife for its own sake, we must broaden the base of support for conservation.

We must, as well, restore the excitement and vigor of the conservation movement. We conservationists are an aging community. Young folks these days who want to make the world a better place are heading for economic and social justice solutions. We must re-engage young people with the joys of natural areas. We need to get the young people engaged in outdoor sports, like climbing and skiing, to become spokespeople for national conservation and recreation corridors.

4. Partners In A "Bigger Tent?"

"It must be considered that there is nothing more difficult to carry out, nor more doubtful of success, nor more dangerous to handle, than to initiate a new order of things. . . . [the majority] do not truly believe in anything new until they have had actual experience of it."

—FROM "THE PRINCE" BY NICCOLO MACHIAVELLI

The distinguishing quality of a national conservation and recreation corridors campaign is its inclusiveness. The theme of the corridors campaign should be straightforwardly nonpartisan and economically mainstream, but with real standards of land health. When many sectors and institutions perceive that a corridors campaign will benefit them, they will board the train. The passengers ought to include:

- **Conservation-minded land-owners,** who could profit

from more campers, anglers, and others interested in adventure

- **Rural communities,** including business leaders, county commissioners, Rotarians, and chambers of commerce
- For-profit **ecological restoration companies** because many riparian areas, grasslands, streams, and derelict farmlands will require rehabilitation
- **Publishers** such as Island Press and the National Geographic Society
- **Manufacturers and retailers** of outdoor gear, such as Patagonia and Black Diamond
- **Recreation-oriented non-profits** such as the Sierra Club, the Audubon Society, trails groups, wildflower societies, birding clubs...
- **Advocates of non-motorized backcountry recreation** and adventure sports including paddlers, considerate mountain bikers, and hikers
- **Education organizations and leaders,** particularly those promoting outdoor, experiential, and science education, such as Outward Bound, National Outdoor Leadership School, and the hundreds of related college academic programs
- **Students** of all ages from across the country who would benefit from outdoor experiences (particularly inner city kids who have never seen a dark sky or heard a coyote howl)
- **Climate justice advocates,** led by 350.org, who are demanding cuts in carbon emissions
- **Angling interests** including Trout Unlimited
- **State and federal politicians** promoting enterprise and job creation in rural areas.

National corridors will increase the prosperity of communities in the West and in the nation. For example, jobs would be gestated in the service sector and tourism industry, in ecological restoration, and in the construction industry by the building of infrastructure, including wildlife crossings on roads, trails, hut systems, campgrounds, outdoor educational facilities, and lodges at guest-oriented ranches.

Finally, and not least, the campaign is key to maintaining any semblance of extensive wildness and ecological integrity in the Rockies and elsewhere. Lacking biogeographic connectivity, America's globally unique diversity of ecosystems and plant and animal species will be vastly diminished by the end of this century. The good news is that nature needs only a little help to heal itself.

The help is straightforward:

- unfragmented **wildlife/ecological link** (conservation corridor or wildway) from Mexico to Canada allowing **unhindered movement of flora and fauna, including wide-ranging carnivores**
- **designated parks, wilderness, and other natural areas** for the security of foraging, migrating, and dispersing wildlife, and for hikers, naturalists, and other recreationists
- **safe wildlife crossings** on major roads and other infrastructure retrofits to accommodate wildlife movement.

Conclusion

Many cultures and religions counsel *humility* in our actions toward other lifeforms, *gratitude* for nature's beauty, and an ethic of *responsibility* to future generations of all beings. These values, along with the sheer beauty and wonder of the natural world and the joys of exploring it, should guide our weaving back together the web of life in North America. A step in this direction is to reconnect severed landscape arteries in order to restore vigor to wildlife and generous opportunities for human-powered recreation across the West and beyond. We invite readers to share their ideas, through *Rewilding Earth* (rewilding.org), about how to launch this movement.

REWILDING
BOOKSTORE

Maroon Bells in Autumn. © *Evan Cantor*

REWILDING AT MANY SCALES: A BOOK REVIEW ESSAY

BY JOHN MILES

Dave Foreman, in his landmark 2004 book *Rewilding North America: A Vision for Conservation in the 21st Century,* makes a convincing case that "To make protected areas more effective, conservationists must now (1) work on very large landscapes, probably continental in scope, and (2) undertake ecological restoration based on *rewilding.*"[1] He advocated for a science-based approach to protecting and creating a network of "core wild areas, wildlife movement linkages, and compatible use lands to meet habitat needs of wide-ranging species, maintain natural disturbance regimes, and permit dispersal and reestablishment of wildlife following natural events such as fires."[2] Dave was thinking big, though of course he was working at all landscape scales. In 2018, he has been working on a local rewilding project in the Sandia Mountains near his Albuquerque home. Since he wrote this book, much thought and action has been invested in pursuing this vision and some progress made on large scale initiatives like Yellowstone to Yukon (Y2Y), Yellowstone to Uintas (Y to U), and Algonquin to Adirondack (A2A.)

In this essay I address the question of whether rewilding should be seen only as a large-scale effort or whether it should be pursued at many scales; and, in so doing, I highlight recent books that describe what might be considered rewilding at various scales. I do this as a participant in the work of The Rewilding Institute, an

The North American Beaver (Castor canadensis)*, preeminent builder of riparian habitat.* © *Sheri Amsel, exploringnature.org*

organization formed by Dave Foreman to advance his ideas about rewilding North America. If we define *rewilding* only at the large and abstract scale of continental conservation, might we miss an opportunity to connect people at smaller scales to the effort? In their recent book *The Future of Conservation in America: A Chart for Rough Waters,* former National Park Service director Jonathan Jarvis and his science adviser, Gary Machlis, argue that conservation must be made relevant to all Americans as a "foundation for building enduring support for conservation." They define relevance in this context as "when an individual, family, or group makes a personal connection with a physical place that evokes a potent emotional response." My argument here is that rewilding at continental scale, regional scale, even local scale will increase the likelihood of this work becoming relevant to people, especially at smaller scales where people can identify with the results of rewilding. As well, rewilding at any scale contributes to Foreman's vision of rewilding at the large landscape scale, the cumulative effect of rewildings large and small.

My thinking about this was stimulated by my reading of recently published books: Joe Riis, *Yellowstone Migrations* (Seattle, Braided River, 2017); Matthew Kauffman et al, *Wild Migrations: Atlas of Wyoming Ungulates* (Corvallis, Oregon State University Press, 2018); Ben Goldfarb, *Eager: The Surprising Secret Life of Beavers and Why They Matter* (White River Junction, VT: Chelsea Green, 2018); and Scott Freeman, *Tarboo Creek: One Family's Quest to Heal the Land* (Portland, OR: Timber Press, 2018.) All of these books describe, in my view, rewilding. They may not all involve Foreman's core wild areas, but they describe work based on science and efforts to enhance wildlife movement across landscapes. They promote land use compatible with the needs of wide-ranging species. Some of these species, like elk, pronghorn, and mule deer in the Yellowstone region, and salmon in the Pacific Northwest, are very wide-ranging. Beavers may not range widely, but as a keystone species enhancing habitats, they help the wide rangers and restore natural processes on the land.

In *Yellowstone Migrations*, photographer Joe Riis presents absolutely stunning photographs of migrating pronghorn, deer, and elk. Research has shown that these ungulates migrate much farther than anyone thought, mule deer and pronghorn all the way from Wyoming's Red Desert to the northern end of the Wyoming Range south of Jackson. The pronghorn migration is the longest land mammal migration in the United States. Elk migrate all over the Greater Yellowstone area; and scientists have mapped their routes. All of the migrations are fraught with peril. *Yellowstone Migrations* photos graphically document the need for just the sort of rewilding Dave Foreman advocates. In the core essay of this book, titled "A New Vision for Yellowstone: An Ecosystem Defined by Migration," environmental journalist Emilene Ostlind provides a history of and primer on migration ecology, a landscape-scale emphasis on wildlife ecology that has recently increased understanding of the nature and importance of migrations. Scientists have mapped migration routes of ungulates in the greater Yellowstone Ecosystem using thousands of GPS coordinates collected by researchers. *Yellowstone Migrations* describes in text, maps, and especially in photographs, migration routes of elk, mule deer, and pronghorn.

After enjoying Riis's photography and the brief essays in *Yellowstone Migrations,* I turned to the definitive work on the Wyoming Migration Initiative by Matthew J. Kauffman and colleagues titled *Wild Migrations: Atlas of Wyoming's Ungulates*. Wildlife ecologist Kauffman, studying herbivory and predation in Yellowstone, became aware that migration of ungulates in the area was a big story that needed research to understand many wildlife dynamics in the region.

"Working with my graduate students, we learned how drought was reducing the forage available to migratory elk near Cody, Wyoming, and how the small herd of Teton sheep had lost its migration. And we were starting to understand how changes to Wyoming's landscapes were making the migrations more difficult. Migrating wildlife need vast swaths of connected habitat. Even now, we don't know how many holes we can punch in these corridors before migrating wildlife will abandon their traditional movements, but we are certain that ever-expanding roads, fences, houses, and well pads make it harder for animals to migrate and reduce the benefits these seasonal journeys provide."[3]

The challenge was to precisely map the migration routes to identify threats and plan conservation actions that might allow the migrations to be sustained. Kauffman decided an atlas was the ideal way to report on the migration research because such a reference "would show where migrations remained intact and where work would be needed to protect them." He emphasized *reference* because the information gathered would not just be of academic interest but also accessible to agencies, conservation groups, transportation planners, and oil and gas developers, among others.

The atlas is a remarkable publication, its large format profusely illustrated with maps, graphs, charts, and brief explanatory text accompanying them. It is divided into sections: background on migration and the animals studied, history, science, threats, and conservation. The migration maps are stunning. For instance, one map of mule deer migrations presents routes between Le Barge, Wyoming and the northern Salt River Range, and includes winter and summer ranges, stopovers, and low and high use corridors. Researchers put collars on 35 deer and collected 5 to 12 data points daily year-round, building a huge database. Researchers organized and analyzed the database, and GIS cartographers present it in astonishing map form.

The importance of this work for rewilding is obvious. The more we know where the migration corridors are, the better we will be able to protect them. Definitive migration maps will provide strong rationales for conservation in the corridors. The most exciting quality of the atlas and the work behind it is the new methodologies it demonstrates, tools for rewilding that were not very advanced when Foreman wrote *Rewilding North America*. Corridors for connectivity, dispersal, and migration are the cornerstone of rewilding—allowing wildlife to roam across landscapes. Discovery of long migration routes adds to understanding of the importance of corridors. It also adds to relevance as defined above, because people living around such corridors can see them on the land, be they citizen conservationists, sportsmen, or even developers. One last thought about *Wild Migrations*—while it is a Wyoming atlas, it reveals a need and an opportunity to map wildlife movements across large landscapes. We have the tools; and rewilders need to advocate for more of this type of work.

Moving on down the rewilding scale, Ben Goldfarb's *Eager: The Surprising, Secret Life of Beavers and Why They Matter,* describes the decline and restoration of the beaver on American lands (and a bit of Europe). Traveling North America from Canada to New Mexico, from Massachusetts to Oregon, Goldfarb recounts how *Castor canadensis* has been trapped to near extinction, rallied and returned only to be considered a nuisance and trapped again. He explains the history of the great aquatic rodent's resilience, how it has recently exceeded what he calls the "cultural carrying capacity" in many places, and various responses people have made to the damage it is perceived they do. He also explains how the beaver can do much good for natural systems across its range, and the many efforts "beaver believers" have made to restore the beaver as a way to rejuvenate waterways. He describes the cascading ecological effects beavers can have on natural systems that were degraded by their past removal.

Relative to rewilding, Goldfarb quotes George Monbiot who, in his book *Feral,* defines rewilding as a recognition that "nature consists not just of a collection of species but also of their ever-shifting relationships with each other and with the physical environment." Goldfarb writes that "Fundamental to Monbiot's version of rewilding is allowing ecosystems to shape their own destinies, rather than micromanaging them. By that standard, beavers, which drive ecological processes like no other creature and bend to no person's will, are rewilding's poster species."[4] Rewilding is not a major theme of Goldfarb's book, but it clearly demonstrates how restoration of a keystone species across many landscapes can be a powerful building block in restoring and protecting wildlife habitat essential to the rewilding process.

The final book in this review takes rewilding to a very local level, which is often how beavers play into the picture. In fact, in Scott Freeman's *Saving Tarboo Creek,* beavers play a role in the long project to restore this salmon-bearing stream on Washington's Olympic Peninsula. Tarboo Creek, only 7.5 miles long, was ditched or diverted and its surrounding wetlands drained. Salmon once ran into the creek to spawn, but disturbances of natural stream flow then blocked their entry. Scott Freeman and his wife Susan, a granddaughter of Aldo Leopold, bought an 18-acre parcel that straddled the creek, and inspired by Aldo's example in Wisconsin, set out to restore the creek. First, they restored meanders, hiring an excavator experienced in such work. They put down coir to control erosion of the freshly cut banks, then turned water into the reengineered stream. They planted trees, aware that in restoring the stream they were "fighting a thousand years of history."[5]

Biologist Freeman, his wife Susan, and family and friends, who all pitched in to do the muddy work on the land, watched the stream heal and salmon return. The Freemans bought a tract of forest near the creek in honor of Carl Leopold, Aldo's son and Susan's father who had helped with the project and passed in 2009. As the work on the creek progressed over the years, beavers returned and started cutting the trees that the restoration crew had so laboriously planted. This posed a problem, but Freeman writes, "if your goal is to live with the land instead of just on it, you have to accept the organisms that live there more or less on their own terms." They wrapped trees they wished to save, and eventually the beavers dammed the creek and created a pond. Freeman writes:

"So beavers are now a feature. The pond they created drowned big trees and shrubs we enjoyed, and even some we planted, but the deaths created snags that attract pileated woodpeckers and red-breasted sapsuckers. The open water has brought in kingfishers, great blue herons, mallards, and wood ducks; it's a paradise for frogs and aquatic insects."[6]

Over the 18 years of their project on Tarboo Creek, nature's resilience has been clear. Freeman further observes:

"If you were designing the perfect salmon stream, then it would start with long stretches of relatively fast-moving water close to the headwaters that provide gravelly spawning habitat. Downstream, there would be even longer stretches of rearing habitat, with a meandering channel broken by a series of beaver ponds."[7]

Tarboo Creek is an example of rewilding at a small scale. Perhaps it involves a bit more micromanaging than Monbiot would approve, but the Freemans demonstrate in their project a local rewilding that became very relevant, in the sense mentioned earlier, to many people in the area.

Just as I think wildness and wilderness exist at many landscape scales, so I think we rewilders should think of work that can be done for rewilding on similar scales. The recent books mentioned in this essay demonstrate that the work of rewilding is in fact occurring at many scales, but it is perhaps not perceived as part of the grand rewilding project as presented in Dave Foreman's *Rewilding North America*. My view is that if rewilding is to be achieved, it must be sought at every opportunity whether that be on the scale of Wyoming or of beavers in Tarboo Creek and other streams across North America. Concluding his book, Ben Goldfarb observes that "Beavers have thoroughly colonized many of our landscapes; reaping the full benefits of their transformative powers will require coexisting with them on millions of acres more." He quotes the author J.B. MacKinnon who wrote, "The conservation of the common represents a deeper ambition than the 20th century's lopsided division of the world into islands of wild. . . . It calls on us to integrate conservation into every aspect of human life." A large order, but rewilding can and must be a part of this.

---

1 Dave Foreman, *Rewilding North America: A Vision for Conservation in the 21st Century*. Washington, D.C.: Island Press, 2004, p. 4.

2 Ibid.

3 Matthew J. Kauffman, Preface, *Wild Migrations,* p. xvi.

4 Ben Goldfarb, *Eager: The Surprising, Secret Life of Beavers and Why They Matter*, p. 217.

5 Scott Freeman, *Saving Tarboo Creek: One Family's Quest to Heal the Land*, p. 77.

6 *Saving Tarboo Creek*, p.149.

7 *Saving Tarboo Creek*, p. 148.

APPENDIX

ABOUT THE COVER

The cover artwork by Evan Cantor titled "Trappers Lake After the Fire" celebrates a notable place and moment in American conservation history.

Colorado's Trappers Lake played an important role in wilderness preservation in America. In 1919, Arthur H. Carhart, the U.S. Forest Service's first landscape architect, was ordered to survey 100 summer home sites and a road around the lake. He carried out his assigned task but concluded his report arguing that the place was too beautiful and wild to be developed: "There are a number of places with scenic value of such great worth that they are rightfully the property of all people. They should be preserved for all time for the people of the nation and the world. Trappers Lake is unquestionably a candidate for that classification."

Early in 1920, the District II Forester designated Trappers Lake to be kept roadless and undeveloped, a small beginning of the movement by the Forest Service toward wilderness preservation. Carhart shared his ideas with Aldo Leopold, who went on to establish the first national forest wilderness, the Gila Wilderness in New Mexico. The National Wilderness Preservation System that ultimately resulted from Carhart and Leopold's idea and action today encompasses 109,000,000 acres and is growing.

ABOUT THE CONTRIBUTORS

Sheri Amsel has written and illustrated more than 25 children's books and field guides. In 2009, she was awarded the Elizabeth Abernathy Hull Award for *Outstanding Contributions to the Environmental Education of Youths*, by the Garden Club of America. Her work has moved online with exploringnture.org, a comprehensive illustrated science resource website for students, educators, and homeschool families. Sheri works out of her home studio in the Adirondacks.

Tim Anderson, Jr. is from Chillicothe, Ohio, where in 2015 he began using drones to capture aerial photos of local landmarks and events.

Jo Ann Baumgartner is executive director of Wild Farm Alliance. She is the co-author of *Supporting Beneficial Birds and Managing Pest Birds and of Biodiversity Conservation: An Organic Farmer's and Certifier's Guide*. Jo Ann co-edited, with Dan Imhoff, Farming and the Fate of Wild Nature: Essays in Conservation-Based Agriculture. Before joining WFA in 2001, she worked for other sustainable agricultural nonprofits, was senior researcher for a book of California's rare wildlife species, and was an organic farmer for over a decade. She has a keen interest in the conservation of native species for their own sake, and the connections between farms and the larger ecosystem.

Douglas Bevington directs Environment Now's programs to protect California's forests. Environment Now recently merged with the Lionardo DiCaprio Foundation.

Dr. Bevington is the author of *The Rebirth of Environmentalism: Grassroots Activism from the Spotted Owl to the Polar Bear* (Island Press, 2009), which chronicles the powerful impact of grassroots forest and biodiversity protection groups on environmental policies in the United States over the past two decades. He holds a PhD in sociology from the University of California, Santa Cruz, where he taught courses on social movement studies.

Dr. Bevington previously worked as the regional organizer for the John Muir Project of Earth Island Institute and as the biodiversity program assistant for the Foundation for Deep Ecology. He has also been active with the Bay Area Coalition for Headwaters, Center for Biological Diversity, Endangered Species Coalition, and Sierra Club. He has served on the board of advisors of the Student Environmental Center and is currently on the board of directors of the Fund for Wild Nature.

Karen Boeger is a retired school teacher, Nevada "Desert Rat," and conservation activist for over 40 years. She loves to hike, ski, canoe & forage. Karen feels fortunate to have grown up at a time when much of the West was still wild and the dominant recreational uses were traditional human powered ones. Within her generation, those opportunities have vastly diminished. She works to ensure that future generations will continue to have the same wilderness opportunities and traditional outback experiences that she has been fortunate to enjoy.

Sean F. Boggs is a commercial photographer out of central Colorado who shoots at least 10% of every year for nonprofits including the EDF, Wounded Warriors, Healing Waters, and ninash.org. He's a cultural adventurer and a genuinely kind person. Mixing that with 35 years of studies and experience in photography and film making is what makes his imagery so powerful. Check him out at Sean F. Boggs on Facebook and Instagram or seanfboggs.com.

Kelly Burke cofounded Grand Canyon Wildlands Council with Kim Crumbo and ecologist Larry Stevens in 1996 and is now executive director of Wild Arizona. She has 14 years' experience in geological mapping, including extensive trips on the Colorado River to advance ecological research and riparian restoration. Kelly has led natural history tours in Grand Canyon, Zion, and Bryce Canyon National Parks, and also in Alaska, and has published scientific articles about structural geology, geomorphology, and geochemistry of natural waters. In 2016, Kelly initiated the Conservation in Motion program to bring together conservationists, scientists, artists, adventurers and outdoor-brand athlete ambassadors in the campaign to permanently protect the lands embracing the north and south rims of Grand Canyon. She lives at the foot of the San Francisco peaks in Flagstaff, where she tries to weave horseback riding and time in the wild with her terrier mix, Georgia, into every reasonably nice day.

Darren Burkey has been creating wildlife art for a long time. Protecting wildlife and their environment has always been a passion of his. Sharing his art with others helps to spread awareness that what we do on a daily basis impacts the ecosystem. He reminds us if we're looking for something exciting to do in the winter, we should take a trip to Jackson, WY and spend time visiting the Elk Refuge - the experience will leave a lasting impact. He's honored to be a contributing artist for Wild/Rewilding Earth and will continue to advocate for protecting what matters most.

Evan Cantor is a long-time Colorado wilderness artist. His works are impressionistic windows into the wilderness places he loves and hopes to protect, images that capture the sacredness of the earth through landscape. These images are informed not only by his own experiences back-of-beyond, but by transcendental philosophies ranging from Thoreau and Whitman to Aldo Leopold and Edward Abbey. Each image represents a place of personal significance and connection to the artist.

Conservationists will recall Evan's scratchboard drawings in *Wild Earth* and *Wildflower* magazines as well as in *High Country News*. His images appeared in several of John Fielder's books published by Westcliffe, and in a number of university presses, the Rocky Mountain Land Library, Southern Rockies Wildlands Network and the Northwest Earth Institute. Exhibitions have included the Arts & Letters Club of Toronto, various juried shows, the National Center for Atmospheric Research and "The Lure of The Local", curated by Lucy Lippard. He is a member of the Temagami 22, an invitational group of North-American artists concerned with environmental preservation and was the Rocky Mountain Land Library's 2005 artist-in-residence. In 2006 he was honored with an award from the Southern Rockies Conservation Alliance for his "outstanding contribution" of both art and music to the wilderness preservation effort in Colorado. He took up oil painting at Ghost Ranch in October 2016 and has been going strong ever since. Evan is also the lead singer of the classic-rock outfit The CBDs, playing the guitar and blues harp.

Sandra Coveny (sandra.coveny@gmail.com; linkedin. com/in/sandracoveny) lives in Oregon, and works as the Soil Scientist and Climate Change Adaptation Planner for The Confederated Tribes of Warm Springs. Sandra is also a freelance writer and applied conservation biologist, and works in service to resilient communities of all kinds, with emphasis on local communities and tribes. The tools of her trade include writing, community organizing, GIS, and landscape-scale restoration planning and implementation.

Some of Sandra's recent projects include forming a new collaborative organization whose mission is in service to traditional knowledge and data sovereignty for tribal communities working toward resiliency in the face of climate change; preparing an outline for climate change adaptation strategy and drought response plan framework for the Montana Department of Natural Resources; convening the first Traditional Knowledge and Climate Change forum at the Society for Conservation GIS annual conference (Monterey, CA July 2018); and, together with Wildlife Institute of India, forming the Society for Conservation GIS India Chapter (August 2018).

John Davis (john@rewilding.org) is executive director of The Rewilding Institute and editor of *Rewilding Earth*. He rounds out his living with conservation field work, particularly within New York's Adirondack Park, where he lives. John serves on boards of RESTORE: The North Woods, Eddy Foundation, Champlain Area Trails, Cougar Rewilding Foundation, and Algonquin to Adirondack Conservation Collaborative. He is the author of *Big, Wild, and Connected: Scouting an Eastern Wildway from Florida to Quebec* and *Split Rock Wildway: Scouting the Adirondack Park's Most Diverse Wildlife Corridor*.

Sara Fern Fitzsimmons has worked at Penn State University with The American Chestnut Foundation since 2003, assisting chestnut growers and researchers throughout the Appalachian Mountains. Born and raised in Hinton, West Virginia, Sara studied Biology at Drew University in Madison, NJ. She then received a Master's degree in forest ecology and resource management from Duke University's Nicholas School. After a short stint as an editorial assistant at *All About Beer Magazine,* Sara returned to the forestry field, where she has been ever since. Sara hopes her research and professional work will facilitate long-term conservation and restoration of native tree species at risk from exotic pests and diseases.

Dave Foreman is a legendary conservation leader and wilderness strategist. His half-century career in conservation has changed, and bettered, the course of the wilderness movement.

Dave's professional work in conservation has included serving as Southwest regional representative for The Wilderness Society [1973-1980], co-founder of Earth First! [1980], publisher of *Wild Earth* magazine (1990-2005), co-founder of The Wildlands Project (1991), co-founder of the New Mexico Wilderness Alliance (1997), and founder of The Rewilding Institute (2003). In these capacities, Dave has coined the phrases and articulated the concepts behind Earth First!, No Compromise in Defense of Mother Earth, Rewilding, and Born to Rewild. He has officiated the marriage between wildlands advocacy and conservation biology. He has empowered the conservation community to think BIG, to strive to protect and restore the whole biotic community, not settle for preserving a few remaining scraps.

Among Dave Foreman's many outstanding conservation accomplishments are getting big additions to the Gila and other Wilderness Areas, blocking numerous timber sales in National Forests, blockading logging roads into various old-growth forests, forcing the Forest Service to re-do its inadequate Roadless Area Review and Evaluation, serving as lead author on several wildlands network designs, founding *Wild Earth* magazine, and getting *rewilding* adopted as a fundamental goal in conservation. Dave received the 1996 Paul Petzoldt Award for Excellence in Wilderness Education and was recognized by Audubon Magazine in 1998 as one of the 20th century's most important conservation leaders.

Dave has shared his visionary ideas on big connected wild places complete with top carnivores through hellfire & brimstone public sermons and through his books. Dave's books include such landmarks as *The Big Outside* (the first road-free areas inventory since Bob Marshall's a half century earlier), *Confessions of an Eco-Warrior, Rewilding North America, Man Swarm*, and *The Great Conservation Divide* (all available through rewilding.org).

Sofia Heinonen is the conservation director for Conservation Land Trust in Argentina, part of the larger Tompkins Conservation team. With Kris Tompkins and her late husband Doug Tompkins, Sofia has helped save hundreds of thousands of acres of wildlands in Argentina, and overseen the reintroduction of several extirpated species, including lowland tapir, pampas deer, and collared peccary. Sofia has a commending knowledge of Argentine ecosystems and how to protect them.

Steven Kellogg graduated from the Rhode Island School of Design in 1963, and forty years later the college presented him with their annual award for significant professional achievement.

He is the acclaimed illustrator and author of more than a hundred picture books, and is a recipient of the prestigious Regina Medal for his lifetime contribution to children's literature. Among the titles he has published are: *Johnny Appleseed, The Mysterious Tadpole, Snowflakes Fall, How much is a Million?,* and *The Word Pirates.*

John Laundré was born and raised in the Midwest (Wisconsin) and received his bachelors and masters degrees there. He received his PhD from Idaho State University in 1979. Since then, he has been working in large mammal predator-prey ecology and has studied predators and their prey in the western U.S. and northern Mexico. His experience includes working with cougars, wolves, coyotes, bobcats, deer, elk, bison, and bighorn sheep. He has conducted one of the longest (17 years) studies of cougar ecology and behavior to date and has published over 80 scientific articles on his scientific work. He is the originator of the concept of the *landscape of fear* which proposed that fear of prey for their predators drives many ecological processes. An important aspect of this concept is that predators are instrumental in maintaining the balance between prey species and their habitat, not so much by killing their prey but affecting how they use the landscape. He is the author of the book, *Phantoms of the Prairie, The Return of Cougars to the Midwest,* that looks at the phenomenon of cougars actually moving back into the Great Plains region of the U.S. He currently lives in western Oregon where he is "semi-retired" and teaching part-time at Western Oregon University. He on the board of the Cougar Rewilding Foundation whose goal is the eventual re-establishment of viable cougar populations in the Eastern U.S.

Gary Lawless is a poet, bioregional advocate, and co-founder of Gulf of Maine Books, in Brunswick Maine. He and his wife Beth Leonard care-take the old farm of Henry Beston & Elizabeth Coatsworth (both acclaimed authors of the mid-20th century), near Damariscotta Lake. Gary's score of poetry collections includes *Poems for the Wild Earth* and *Caribou Planet.*

His new book of poems is *How the Stones Came to Venice,* and his poetry blog is mygrations.blogspot.com.

Nancy Lehrhart has been an outdoor and nature enthusiast since childhood. She met and married John "Obie" Oberhausen and together with their best friend, Joe Newman, formed The Cactus Rescue Project. A Nurse Practitioner for 30 years, Nancy has an affinity for plants and people that need a helping hand. She is one of the founding members of the Eldorado School and Community Garden, a past organizer of the Eldorado Gardening Tour and has taught classes on home gardening. She and Obie have worked long hours on their extensive home cactus garden which has been the subject of tours for many different local groups and organizations.

Jon Leibowitz is the Executive Director of the Northeast Wilderness Trust, based in Montpelier, Vermont. Prior to joining the Wilderness Trust, he served as the Executive Director of the Montezuma Land Conservancy in the Four Corners region of Colorado. During his time at Montezuma Land Conservancy, he protected over 13,000 acres of farms and ranchland and spearheaded an effort to expand conservation to include outdoor focused educational programming. Joining the Wilderness Trust is a return to New England for Jon and his family. He earned a Masters in Environmental Law and Policy and a Juris Doctor from Vermont Law School.

Bob Leverett is the co-founder of the Native Tree Society, co-founder and President of Friends of Mohawk Trail State Forest, chairperson for the Massachusetts Department of Conservation and Recreation Forest Reserves Scientific Advisory Committee, and the co-author of the American Forests Champion Tree-Measuring Guidelines handbook. He is also co-author of several books including the *Sierra Club Guide to Ancient Forests of the Northeast, Old Growth in the East, a Survey, Eastern Old Growth Forest – Prospects for Rediscovery and Recovery, and Wilderness Comes Home – Re-Wilding the Northeast.* Educated as an engineer, Bob is a recognized expert in the science of measuring trees for both science and sport. His association with old-growth forest discoveries and confirmations dates to the middle 1980s.This compelling interest placed him in the center of the early old growth preservation movements, which continue to this day.

Robert Leverett, son of the East's preeminent old-growth sleuth Bob Leverett, carries on the family tradition of finding and protecting big old trees. Rob is rooted in Native American traditions, and teaches flint-napping as well as exploring and sketching old-growth forests. Rob lives and rambles in New York's Adirondack Park, where old-growth forest still comprises much of the landscape.

Roderick MacIver's art is inspired by canoe trips in the Canadian north, by time in the Adirondack woods, by a quiet life on the outside looking in. Birdsong, a few good friends, paddling wild rivers. Painting. In 1994, he founded Heron Dance, a newsletter then book publisher, that explored the human search for meaning, the human connection to the natural world and creativity. Rod retired from Heron Dance a few years ago, but copies remain of his remain. Rod believes that perhaps each human life is fed by the underground spring of a few experiences, that when we are there, we touch something beyond words, and that they make us who we are.

Lucila Masera studied chemical engineering in Buenos Aires, and environmental engineering in Madrid, where she also worked in a forestry consulting firm for 2 years. In 2017 she started working at CLT, where she was one of the co-founders of the marine conservation program with the objective of protecting at least 10% of the Argentine Sea. In 2018, she became director of strategy and development.

Larry Master is a conservation biologist, a zoologist, and, in his retirement, a conservation photographer. He has been photographing wildlife and natural history subjects for more than 60 years. After doctoral and post-doctoral studies at the University of Michigan, Larry spent 20 years with The Nature Conservancy (TNC) and 6 years with NatureServe, most of that time as their Chief Zoologist. NatureServe is an offshoot of the Conservancy and is the umbrella organization for the network of natural heritage programs and conservation data centers in every U.S. state and Canadian province as well as in many Latin American countries. Larry started several of these programs (e.g., MI, NH, VT) and also oversaw the development of TNC's and NatureServe's central zoological databases and revisions to the Network's Conservation Status Assessment methodology. He also served on EPA's Science Advisory Board. Larry conceived and co-authored *Rivers of Life: Critical Watersheds for Protecting Freshwater Biodiversity*. He has also authored numerous articles as well as chapters in several books (e.g., *Precious Heritage, Our Living Resources*). In his retirement he serves on boards of the *Adirondack Explorer,* the Ausable River Association, and the Northern Forest Atlas Foundation, as well as on the Center for Ecostudies Science Advisory Council, The Biodiversity Conservancy's Advisory Board, NatureServe's Strategic Advisors Council, and the American Society of Mammalogists' Mammal Images Library. Larry resides in Keene, NY and West Cornwall, CT.

Tim McNulty is a poet, essayist, and nature writer based on Washington's Olympic Peninsula. He is the author of ten poetry books and eleven books of natural history. Tim has received the Washington State Book Award and the National Outdoor Book Award among other honors. Tim's newest book of poems, *Ascendance*, is published by Pleasure Boat Studio. His natural history books include *Olympic National Park: A Natural History,* and *Washington's Mount Rainier National Park*. His work has been translated into German, Chinese, and Japanese. Tim lives with his wife in the foothills of the Olympic Mountains.

Brad Meiklejohn has worked with The Conservation Fund since 1994, where he has directed conservation projects protecting over 300,000 acres of wild land in Alaska, New Hampshire and Nevada. Brad is also a director of the American Packrafting Association, with over 2,000 members in 30 countries, and has completed packraft expeditions on 6 continents. Brad served as Associate Director for the Utah Avalanche Center during the 1980s, and as President of the Patagonia Land Trust. Brad is a past board director of The Murie Center and the Alaska Avalanche School.

John Miles grew up in New Hampshire and graduated from Dartmouth College with a degree in anthropology. He earned an MA at the University of Oregon in Recreation and Park Management and a PhD in Environmental Studies and Education at the Union Institute. While at Dartmouth, John attended a talk by David Brower, then Executive Director of the Sierra Club, who spoke about the threat of dams to Grand Canyon National Park. Inspired by Brower's talk and books such as Stewart Udall's *The Quiet Crisis,* John was hooked.

After grad school he landed in Bellingham, Washington where he became involved in his first conservation issue, the establishment of North Cascades National Park. At Western Washington University, John was in on the founding of Huxley College of Environmental Studies, where he taught environmental education, history, ethics, and literature, and ultimately served as dean of the College. He taught at Huxley for 44 years, climbing and hiking all over the West, especially in the North Cascades, for research and recreation. Author and editor of several books, including *Guardians of the Parks, Koma Kulshan, and Wilderness in National Parks,* John served on the board of the National Parks Conservation Association and the Washington Forest Practices Board, and he helped found and build the North Cascades Institute.

Retired now and living with his wife Susan Morgan near Taos, New Mexico, John continues to work on national parks, wilderness, and rewilding the earth, and he hikes, bikes, and skis whenever possible. He contributes to the websites rewilding.org and nationalparkstraveler.org and is writing a history of the North Cascades Institute.

Susan Morgan, PhD, studied Southwest archaeology and holds degrees in English and environmental studies. In 1967 she began as Director of Education for The Wilderness Society where she worked for over ten years and has subsequently worked in education and outreach positions with wilderness, wildlands, and public lands conservation organizations. She is currently president of The Rewilding Institute and senior editor of *Rewilding Earth.*

Sherry Nemmers is an advocate for cats and other animals, wild and domestic. As Executive Creative Director and Executive Vice President of NYC-based global ad agencies for over three decades, Sherry created icons for world leaders such as Procter & Gamble, Toyota, Ad Council, General Mills and Mars, Inc., among others. As an example, Sherry created the Charmin Bears for Charmin bath tissue, and created the award-winning crime prevention icon, McGruff the Crime Dog. She has garnered over 500 awards, including The One Show, Effies, Pinnacle, and the prestigious INSPIRE award given for outstanding leadership and innovation, which P&G created in her honor. Sherry has been interviewed on *NBC Dateline, CBS Sunday Morning, CNN, WSJ, NYTimes, NYSun, Adweek*, among others, and teaches at industry seminars. Sherry serves on Boards for the Adirondack Council, the Adirondack Lake Center for the Arts, SpayFirst, and is an active alum and class officer for Vassar College. She divides her time between New York City and Blue Mountain Lake, among music, horses, cats, wildlife and wildlands.

Fred Paillet is adjunct professor at the University of Arkansas, where he conducts research and supervises student projects related to geophysics, hydrology and paleoecology. After retiring from the U. S. Geological Survey's National Research Program in 2002 he held temporary appointments at the University of Maine and the University of Rennes (France), before moving to Arkansas in 2009. He has participated in long-term studies at the Hubbard Brook Experimental Forest in New Hampshire and other field sites, resulting in several books along with numerous journal articles and other technical publications.

David R. Parsons got his Bachelor of Science degree in Fisheries and Wildlife Biology from Iowa State University and his Master of Science degree in Wildlife Ecology from Oregon State University. Dave is retired from the U.S. Fish and Wildlife Service where from 1990-1999 he led the effort to reintroduce the endangered Mexican gray wolf to the American Southwest. Dave's interests include the ecology and conservation of large carnivores, protection of biodiversity, and wildlands conservation at scales that fully support ecological and evolutionary processes. He is the Carnivore Conservation Biologist for The Rewilding Institute, a member of the Science Advisory Board of Project Coyote, a former member and chairman of the Board of Directors of the New Mexico Wilderness Alliance, and a former graduate advisor in the Environmental Studies master's degree program at Prescott College. Dave serves as a science and policy advisor for organizations and coalitions advocating for wolf recovery and landscape-scale conservation in the Southwest.

In 2001, Dave received the New Mexico Chapter of The Wildlife Society's annual "Professional Award." In 2007 at the North American Wolf Conference, Dave received the "Alpha Award" for his "outstanding professional achievement and leadership toward the recovery of Mexican wolves." In 2008 Dave received the "Outstanding Conservation Leadership Award" from the Wilburforce Foundation and the "Mike Seidman Memorial Award" from the Sky Island Alliance for his conservation achievements.

Dave enjoys wildlife viewing, wilderness adventures, and dancing. He lives in Albuquerque, NM, with his wife, Noralyn.

Kevin Raines earned an MFA in Painting from Concordia University in Montreal in 1979 and returned to the States to work as a figurative artist, commission portrait painter, illustrator, and Professor of Art at Notre Dame of Maryland University. A New York resident, he lives and works in Maryland and the Adirondacks. Drawing his inspiration from the beauty of the landscape and his passion for conservation, he has worked closely with local and international conservation science agencies for over 35 years to promote public awareness of our natural environment. Kevin's beautiful painting of Split Rock Wildway from the summit of Coon Mountain is on the cover of *Split Rock Wildway: Scouting the Adirondack Park's Most Diverse Wildlife Corridor* (available from Rewilding Bookstore).

Matias Rebak (matiasrebak@gmail.com) is a lawyer and a photographer who works for the Iberá National Park and Comité Iberá in Corrientes. He also collaborates voluntarily with the Conservation Land Trust Argentina. Matias bought his first camera for a trip to India and Nepal because he wanted to photograph everything that happened before his eyes. He has never taken a photography course so considers himself a self-taught photographer, however learning all the time from friends who are great photographers. Matias takes photos of nature, wildlife, and adventure racers in forests and mountains.

Kirk Robinson is the founder and executive director of the Western Wildlife Conservancy, a non-profit wildlife conservation organization (westernwildlifeconservancy.org). He lives in Salt Lake City, Utah. Prior to founding Western Wildlife Conservancy, Kirk earned a Ph.D. in philosophy and taught courses at universities in Montana and Utah for 15 years. He also has a J.D. with a certificate in natural resource law. His favorite activities are exploring the wildlands and rivers of the American West and playing acoustic guitar.

Nicole Rosmarino helped found the Southern Plains Land Trust and is currently its Executive Director. She served as the caretaker for SPLT-protected land from 1999-2002, during which time she monitored for trespass and to record flora and fauna observed several times per week, while residing in Pritchett, Colorado. She now resides in Centennial, CO. Nicole received her Ph.D. from the University of Colorado at Boulder in May 2002. Her Ph.D. is in policy science/political science, and her academic focus was on biodiversity preservation. She has been actively involved in efforts to protect prairie wildlife since 1994.

Robin Silver is one of the Center for Biological Diversity's founders. A retired emergency-room physician in Phoenix and a professional wildlife photographer, Robin works on conservation issues in the Southwest with a focus on the San Pedro River.

Terry Spahr (tspahr1@gmail.com) graduated from the University of Pennsylvania with a BA in History and a Master's Degree in Government Administration from Penn's Fels Center of Government. Terry had a successful career in the insurance and investment fields and, most recently, in the real estate brokerage industry as Regional Executive Vice President for Long & Foster Companies, which was until recently the United States' largest privately-owned real estate company. In 2016 Terry left the corporate world and decided to devote his interest in politics, science, and the environment toward researching, writing, and producing *8 Billion Angels* (8BillionAngels.org), a documentary exploring the impact of humanity's growing numbers on planet Earth. The film details mankind's rapid ascent across the globe and the inextricable links between population growth and our ever-increasing food, water, climate, and extinction emergencies. Terry uncovers the truth about climate change, the challenges we face, and the solutions that can work to bring about a sustainable future. Terry lives in Ardmore, PA with his family, including two dogs, a cat and 10,000 bees.

Christopher Spatz is a former president of the Cougar Rewilding Foundation and a director of the Gunks Climbers' Coalition. He writes and lectures about the natural history of the Catskill Mountains and the Shawangunk Ridge in southern New York State, where he lives and where he caught the spell of the fabled eastern cougar.

Michael Soulé is often called the father of conservation biology. Michael co-founded several key groups, including the Society for Conservation Biology and The Wildlands Project (now Wildlands Network). He is the author or editor of countless articles and books, including *Continental Conservation* (co-edited with John Terborgh). Along with being a world-renowned biologist, Michael is a philosopher who studied with Deep Ecology formulator Arne Naess and in recent years has been studying the concept of *sin*, and what it tells us about the extinction crisis.

Nancy Stranahan serves as the Director of the Arc of Appalachia Preserve System, and was one of the non-profit's founders in 1995. In the span of directing the organization over the last 20-plus years, Nancy has cultivated a vigorous citizen advocacy network in Ohio, which she refers to as a tree-roots network. The Arc has saved and preserved over 7,000 acres of natural areas in Appalachian Ohio, representing 21 preserve regions and over 100 separate real estate negotiations and fund-raising campaigns. The Arc's headquarters, the 2,500-acre Highlands Nature Sanctuary, is the Arc's largest and oldest preserve region, and is the hub of the Arc's primary visitor services, offering over 16 miles of public hiking trails, overnight lodges, and an interpretive Museum. A few of the many rare and common signature species protected within the Arc suite of nature preserves are Henslow sparrows, cerulean warblers, golden star lilies, northern long-eared bats and timber rattlesnakes. Under Nancy's guidance, the Arc has also been instrumental in saving several 2,000-year old Native American earthwork complexes, notably Spruce Hill, Glenford Fort, Junction, and Steel Earthwork sites. In addition, the Arc manages two long-protected earthwork sites—Fort Hill and Serpent Mound—working as a contract manager for the Ohio History Connection. Previously in her career Nancy served as Chief Naturalist for Ohio State Parks with the Ohio Dept. of Natural Resources; and operated Benevolence Café and Bakery in downtown Columbus for 20 years, where she promoted healthy and intentional food choices.

Kim Vacariu is the former Western Director for Wildlands Network, where he led efforts by the 25-member Western Wildway Network to protect and connect wildlife habitat corridors stretching from Alaska to Mexico. Kim has been instrumental in organizing new partner coalitions, elevating the recognition of habitat connectivity threats posed by the walling off of the U.S.-Mexico borderlands, including organization of the first Border Ecological Symposiums in Arizona. He also convened the first private lands conservation workshops in Arizona, and received the Federal Highway Administration's 2007 Environmental Excellence Award for his work in creating Arizona's statewide Wildlife Linkage Assessment. Kim was co-author in 2,000 of the ground-breaking Sky Islands Wildlands Network Design—the first effort to publish specific science-based maps and implementation steps required for protection of core, corridor and compatible use areas within regional habitat networks. He has authored numerous articles and papers devoted to raising awareness of the importance of large-scale landscape connectivity. He served as Wildlands Network's Communications Director from 1998-2000. Kim founded, edited and published the Steamboat Springs Review (Colorado), a conservation-focused newspaper that received that city's "Shining Star Award" for community environmental service in 1996. Kim works from his home in Portal, Arizona, where he is a board member of Friends of Cave Creek Canyon and organizes an annual "Heritage Days" event focusing on the importance of recognizing wildlife and habitat as critical members of the local community.

Brendan Wiltse is a conservation and nature photographer based in the Adirondack Park of northern New York. His work focuses on connecting people to wild places with the intention of building enthusiasm for supporting wildlands conservation. Brendan is also the Vice President of The Waterman Fund, dedicated to preserving the spirit of wildness in the Northeast. He holds a Ph.D. in biology from Queen's University and is the

Science & Stewardship Director for the Ausable River Association. Brendan's academic focus is on understanding the effects of road salt and climate change on Adirondack lakes and conserving wild brook trout populations.

George Wuerthner is a professional photographer, writer, and ecologist. He has written more than two dozen books on natural history and other environmental topics. He is currently the ED of Public Lands Media, a project of Earth Island Institute. Wuerthner has visited hundreds of mountain ranges around the West, more than 380 wilderness areas, more than 180 national park units, and every national forest west of the Mississippi.

Suzanne York is the Director of Transition Earth. She has reported on international human rights, globalization, and environmental issues for over two decades. Previously Suzanne was Senior Writer and Program Director with the Institute for Population Studies in Berkeley, CA, where her work focused on the interconnectedness of population issues with women's empowerment, human rights, consumption, alternative economies, and the environment. She is the author of several reports, including Peoples' Rights, Planet's Rights: Holistic Approaches to a Sustainable Population and Prioritizing the PHE Approach: Linking Population, Health, and Environment for a Better World. As research director with the International Forum on Globalization, Suzanne was a contributing author to Paradigm Wars: Indigenous Peoples' Resistance to Economic Globalization. She has a Master's Degree in Public Policy from American University and a B.A. in Business Administration from Portland State University.

ABOUT THE REWILDING INSTITUTE AND REWILDING EARTH

The Rewilding Institute (TRI) is a wild bunch of fiercely dedicated conservation activists and scientists who promote and employ strategies to protect, restore, and reconnect wild places and creatures at all scales, across North America and beyond. *Rewilding Earth* is our online publication; and *Rewilding Earth Unplugged* is our annual print anthology comprised of many of its best articles and art.

Rewilding Earth is quickly growing into the publication of record for rewilding projects far and wide, and will soon include a Rewilding Directory, briefly describing and giving contact information for hundreds of projects around the world. We are volunteer-led and reader-supported, so cannot pay for articles or art, but we welcome contributions, literary, artistic, and financial. We especially want to share species recovery and wildways protection success stories and lessons therefrom.

Along with our publications, The Rewilding Institute has several focal on-ground campaigns. These initiatives we help lead (as outlined in parts of this book), even while lending our expertise—soon largely through our nascent Rewilding Leadership Council—to Continental Wildways and species recovery efforts farther afield.

Lobo Recovery – Our Carnivore Conservation Biologist Dave Parsons oversaw the original reintroduction of Mexican wolves into the wilds of southern New Mexico and Arizona as a biologist with the US Fish & Wildlife Service. Dave now leads TRI's advocacy and education work on behalf of Mexican wolves, in partnership with other members of the Mexican Wolf Coalition.

Dave Parsons also serves as advisor to Project Coyote; and we assist that small but mighty group in its efforts to end persecution of predators and ban wildlife-killing contests. We also join efforts with Western Wildlife Conservancy and other good groups to reform state wildlife governance.

Mogollon Wildway – Critical to the long-term prosperity of Lobos and other wide-ranging animals of the Southwest is better protection of the wildlife corridor linking the Gila wildlands complex in southwest New Mexico with the Grand Canyon wildlands complex in northern Arizona. We advocate for the Mogollon Wildway in part by scouting and working with conservation and trail partners to chart a Lobo National Scenic Trail, to popularize the wildlife corridor. Together with groups like New Mexico Wilderness Coalition, Wildlands Network, and Wild Arizona, we push for stronger protections of National Forests and other public lands in Mogollon Wildway.

Puma Recovery for Eastern Wildways – Using ecological, ethical, health, and aesthetic arguments, we promote restoration of the missing top carnivores of the East, including puma and gray and red wolves. Currently, we focus on the puma, or cougar, in concert with Cougar Rewilding Foundation and other carnivore advocacy groups, because its absence means unnaturally high deer numbers and widespread over-browsing of eastern deciduous forests and its reintroduction ought to be achievable in the near term. Many relatively wild parts of the Southeast Coastal Plain, Appalachians, and Adirondacks have good habitat and abundant prey for pumas, but many biologists think it unlikely that pumas will recolonize the East in functional numbers any time soon and that active reintroduction needs to be considered. As with wolves in the West, puma recovery in the East will depend upon building strong public support and reforming state wildlife governance.

Adirondack Wildways – TRI is part of the Eastern Wildway Network formed by Wildlands Network (and informed by Dave Foreman's book *Rewilding North America* and John Davis's book *Big, Wild, and Connected: Scouting an Eastern Wildway from Florida to Quebec).* We pay extra attention to areas we've explored extensively, particularly within New York's great Adirondack Park and habitat connections to surrounding wildlands. Most especially, we work with Northeast Wilderness Trust, Champlain Area Trails, Adirondack Land Trust, Eddy Foundation, and other partners to protect Split Rock Wildway, linking Lake Champlain and its valley with the Adirondack High Peaks. In Split Rock Wildway, we will soon explore with The American Chestnut Foundation the potential for planting disease-resistant American Chestnuts in old fields, as well as native oaks and hickories and other food-rich species that may thrive in a warming climate and may help keep forests resilient in a century of climate chaos. We also work for the Algonquin Park (Ontario) to Adirondack Park wildway, with the A2A collaborative. For the larger Eastern Wildways effort, part of our contribution will be promoting efforts to restore American eel and other diadromous fish populations.

Population – Society cannot avert the overarching crisis of our time—extinction—or the related climate crisis without addressing the fundamental driver of biodiversity loss and greenhouse gas accumulation: too many people consuming too many resources. TRI acknowledges that we humans are billions too many already; and we support compassionate, fair, and effective means of achieving population reduction to ecologically sustainable numbers. We believe that supporting small families, education and empowerment of girls and women, and providing universal access to safe family planning methods, ought to be high priorities for all conservation, environmental, social justice, and peace groups.

Needless to say, we welcome your support for this work of restoring a wild Earth.

Donations can be made online (rewilding.org) or checks mailed to The Rewilding Institute, P.O. Box 13768, Albuquerque, NM 87192.

If you'd like to write an article, please contact John Davis at hemlockrockconservation@gmail.com or Susan Morgan at susancoyote@icloud.com. If you'd like to do a podcast with us, please contact Jack Humphrey at jdh358@gmail.com.

REWILDING EARTH WEBSITE POST INDEX

Below is an index showing all articles that were published on the *Rewilding Earth* website in 2018. Articles are listed by author's last name, followed by the article title. Interested readers will be able to access any articles here by entering either the author's name or the article name in SEARCH near the top right of the main website page at rewilding.org.

Abegao, Jaoa, "The Human Overpopulation Atlas." Abegao has prepared this, his Master thesis in Ecology and Environment, the first of several volumes with the intent on making the case that many of the symptoms of ecological, environmental, sociological, geopolitical and economic predicaments that have tainted our world, have a root cause or can be linked to our vast and rising numbers.

Batrus, Jackie, "Nature Needs Half." This profile is presented by NNH staff and provided by the NNH Community Architect. NNH is an international coalition of scientists, conservationists, nonprofits, and public officials defending nature at the scale she needs to continue to function for the benefit of all life.

Baumgartner, Jo Ann, "Fostering Wildlife-Friendly Farming and Recognizing Biodiversity as Critical to a Fully Functioning Farm." The Executive Director of the Wild Farm Alliance highlights the many benefits of "farming with the wild."

Bevington, Doug, "Forest Protection in the Trump Era." The Director of Forest Programs with Environment Now confronts misinformation used by the Trump administration and points out the opportunity to overcome recent constraints and revitalize broad support for genuine forest protection.

Christian, Logan, "Defending Our Public Lands, Yellowstone to Uintas Connection." Outreach and Development Director of the Y2U Connection, Christian tells the story of extending the 350-mile Yellowstone to Uintas Wildlife corridor between the Greater Yellowstone Ecosystem and Utah's Uinta Mountains that encompasses national parks, monuments, wildlife, and bird refuges and wilderness areas.

Conservation Land Trust, Tompkins Conservation, press release, "Iberá National Park. Established by Argentine Congress." CLT announces the creation of Iberá National Park, located in northeastern Argentina, ensuring long-term conservation of the almost 395,000 acres it encompasses.

Conservation Land Trust, Tompkins Conservation, "Rewilding Argentina and Beyond, Park by Park, Part 1 & 2." Conservation Land Trust Argentina, under the umbrella of Tompkins Conservation initiated to create national parks, sustain biodiversity, restore degraded lands, reintroduce missing species, and encourage environmental activism.

Coveny, Sandra, "The Killing Roads." Coveny is a freelance writer, strategic planner, fundraiser, applied conservation biologist, and climate adaptation planner in service to resilient communities of all kinds, but with emphasis on local communities and tribes.

Davis, John, "Following Alice the Moose, Notes from an A2A Reconnaissance Hike." Davis relates his hike along the Adirondack to Algonquin Wildway. Tracking Alice's route through moose country helps guide our exploration and advocacy work for 2019 and beyond.

Davis, John, "Puma Recovery for Eastern Wildways, Parts 1, 2, 3, & 4." Davis writes that now, in 2018, as we enter a century of climate chaos, only tiny eastern populations persist of the keystone predators who protect forests from over-browsing.

Davis, John and Kelly Burke, "Mogollon Wildway Ramble." Davis and Burke, Grand Canyon Wildlands Council cofounder and map lover write that "Mexican Wolves are trying to return to the Grand Canyon via the Mogollon Wildway. Lone, intrepid lobos have made the journey toward home, setting down four swift paws along the forest pathways out from the heart of their recovery area, in America's Southwest. Yet, deadly highway crossings and the arbitrary boundaries set by wildlife agencies remain serious obstacles to Nature's irrepressible rewilding."

Davis, John, "Split Rock Wildway." Davis, Rewilding Earth editor and Split Rock Wildway steward, describes the area in three parts:

Part 1, "Emplacing a Piece of the Atlantic/Appalachian Wildway."

Part 2, "Adirondack's Most Diverse Wildlife Corridor."

Part 3, "Half Way Home."

Davis, John, "Rewilding Distilled." Davis describes the history and defines the meaning of rewilding.

Dunlop, Charles E.M., "Charles Dunlop Reviews Richard Powers' *The Overstory*." Dunlop, professor emeritus of philosophy, reports Powers' thesis is that humans are destroying the planet because we're both acquisitive by nature and oblivious to the long-term consequences of that impulse.

Eddy Foundation, "Dying Green, How Your Death Can Help Wildlife," introduces the Spirit Sanctuary in Split Rock Wildway, New York.

"Family Portraits." Stunning wildlife photographs by an anonymous contributor.

Fields, Kenyon, "Mountain Island Ranch, Little Dolores - River Restoration Pilot Project, Report 1." Fields, co-manager of Mountain Island Ranch, summarizes the process of studying the logistics, costs, rebound of native vegetation, and efficacy of various methods of removing Russian olive and Tamarisk prior to planning a watershed-wide, multi-year restoration project.

Fitzsimmons, Sara, "Working to Restore the American Chestnut." Fitzsimmons, Director of Restoration, The American

Chestnut Restoration Foundation, writes about efforts underway to restore the American chestnut including traditional breeding methods, simple conservation strategies, methods that reduce the virulence of the blight fungus, and modern genetic transformation techniques.

Foreman, Dave, "The American Public Lands," Chapter 11 from *The Great Conservation Divide.* Foreman, founder of The Rewilding Institute, recounts the history of American public lands from the revolutionary period to the present.

Foreman, Dave, Around the Campfire, #77, "Deconstructing Today's Great Land Grab." Foreman "wants to shoot down the underlying assertions made by the boosters for the Land Grab," including that Federal Public Lands should be returned to the states, that eastern states got a better deal receiving federal lands grants than did western states, and that western states are overburdened by a high percentage of Federal Public Lands.

Gintzler, Ariella, *Outside Magazine,* "Patagonia Fires Another Shot in the Public Lands Battle." Gintzler writes that the clothing company has, once again, come out against the Trump administration for its handling of public lands. He writes about Patagonia taking a strong stand against the Trump administration's onslaught against national monuments and other public lands, and its connections with the energy industry.

Grossman, Richard M.D., "Recognize Family Planning as a Human Right." Grossman is a life-long population control advocate and in this article celebrates his historic presentation at the International Conference on Human Rights, in Tehran, 1968.

Harding, Rob, "A Proposal for a United Nations Framework Convention on Population Growth." Harding is Sustainability Communications Manager at NumbersUSA, a volunteer for the Center for the Advancement of the Steady State Economy, a Great Transition Initiative Champion, and a signer of The Ecological Citizen's Statement of Commitment to Ecocentrism. He proposes to adequately limit population growth, reassess the role of an economy rooted in growth, reduce greenhouse gases, incentivize renewable energy, protect habitat, restore ecosystems, curb pollution, halt defaunation, and constrain invasive alien species.

Harding, Rob, "Population: The Elephant Has Left the Room." Harding writes that population is a primary driver of environmental degradation and a key conservation issue.

Horejsi, Brian, "Extinction: A Deplorable Failure." Dr. Horejsi, retired, describes plummeting numbers of woodland caribou in British Columbia and Idaho, now, in March 2019, declared extinct.

Jepson, Paul, "The Story of a Recoverable Earth." Repost, from *Resurgence and Ecologist*, Issue 311, November-December 2018, All is One, Undercurrent, Jepson, says a new environmental narrative that emphasizes regrowth and possibility could provide the hope we need to make a change.

Johns, David, Review, "*Dark Green Religion* by Bron Taylor." Johns discusses Taylor's thesis that in order for conservation to broadly influence behavior it must become embedded in existing belief systems.

Kerr, Andy, "Using the Bundys for Good: Finding the Silver Lining for Public Lands." Repost of his blog. Kerr, in his Public Land Blog, argues that that the more the Bundys—especially the patriarch, Cliven—talk, the better off are America's public lands.

Kolankiewicz, Leon, reviews "CAPS Talks About the New Edition of Man Swarm." Repost of TRI post, on 2.26.15, Senior Writing Fellow for Californians for Population Stabilization (CAPS), wildlife biologist, and environmental scientist and planner.

Laurance, Bill, "Forest-Destroying Project Drives Environmental and Societal Change." This is an alert containing information and links from the Director of the Centre for Tropical Environmental and Sustainability Science (TESS) and the

Director of the Alliance of Leading Environmental Researchers and Thinkers (ALERT). In this piece, Laurance details China's Belt & Road Project.

Lawless, Gary, "Birds Fly Through the Sacred." Poem. Poet Lawless is a bioregional advocate and founder of Gulf of Maine Books.

Lawless, Gary, "Birds of Greece." Poem.

Lawless, Gary, "The Good News." Poem.

Lehrhaupt, Nancy, Introducing the Santa Fe-Based Cactus Rescue Project, "Rescuing an Endangered Cactus: Restoring the Santa Fe Cholla." Lehrhaupt describes the citizen science effort initiated by Santa Fe "cactusphyles" to locate the cactus in Santa Fe County and replant in protected areas before redistributing them to museums, schools, and gardens.

Leibowitz, Jon, "Safeguarding an Adirondack Wildlife Corridor, for Wildlife and People." The Executive Director of Northeast Wilderness Trust writes about the Split Rock Wildway that connects the fertile lowlands of the Champlain Valley with the rugged High Peaks to the west.

Leverett, Rob, "Eastern Old-Growth Forests, Then and Now." Leverett, founder of The Native Tree Society, old-growth advocate, and writer, summarizes the history of important old-growth forests in the Northeast.

Living with Lions: "Co-existence with an Iconic American Carnivore." This is a notice of a meeting in Sonoma County about the critical roles play in the maintenance and functioning of natural ecosystems with an update of research results by Audubon Canyon Ranch's Wildlife Ecologist.

Maloof, Joan, "Tree Rights Revolution." Maloof, founder and director of the Old-Growth Forest Network works to preserve, protect, and promote the country's few remaining stands of old-growth forest.

McGinnis, Helen, "Introducing Puma Rewilding Profile: KLANDAGI." McGinnis establishes a Facebook account to track puma activities in the Midwest and East outside of FL and to share articles and photos.

McNulty, Tim, "Letter to America, The Elwha: A River and a Vision Restored." McNulty, poet, essayist, and nature writer from Washington's Olympic Peninsula, wrote this letter, a Repost that originally appeared in Terrain.org, and in it describes the dismantling of the Elwha Dam on Washington's Olympic Peninsula and restoration of a wild river.

McNulty, Tim, "Night, Sourdough Mountain Lookout." McNulty, poet, essayist, and nature writer, is the author of three poetry collections, and eleven books on natural history.

Meiklejohn, Brad, "Facing the Challenges of Dam Removal in Alaska." Meiklejohn, describes the near completion of demolition of the long-abandoned Lower Eklutna River dam.

Meiklejohn, Brad, "It's Your Refuge." Meiklejohn, Alaska explorer and conservationist, argues as an Alaskan for preservation of "one of the places on earth that is still intact."

Meiklejohn, Brad, "Bowman Divide Critter Crossing." Meiklejohn advocates for the wildlife corridor near Randolph, New Hampshire, in his father's name.

Miles, John, "The Attack on the National Park System, Parts 1 & 2." Professor Emeritus of Environmental Studies, Western Washington University and long-time parks advocate, discusses multiple threats to National Parks in the Trump Administration from the retreat from science in management.

Part 1: Identifies and describes two major threats, retreat from science and climate change.

Part 2: argues for outdoor recreation compatible with protection of other park values.

Miles, John, "Review, *Firestorm: How Wildfire Will Shape Our Future*, by Edward Struzik." A fellow at the School of Policy Studies, Queen's Institute for Energy and Environmental Policy at Queen University in Kingston, Canada—presents an almost overwhelming array of facts about wildfires that leave room for little doubt about the hazard they represent.

Miles, John, "Book Review Essay, Rewilding at Many Scales." Miles highlights several new books that he suggests deal with rewilding as presented in Rewilding North America but on smaller geographic areas.

Miles, John, "Why States Will Not Serve the American Public as Well as Federal Land Managers." Miles argues that public lands are better protected for the public by the BLM, USFS, and other agencies than would be likely under state management.

Miles, John, "Suggested Reading." This briefly reviews books that relate to wilderness, wildlands, and rewilding that can be updated as new reviews are written or received.

Mountain Lion Foundation Tribute, "Mourning the Loss of Dr. Alan Rabinowitz." Citing Dr. Rabinowitz's life of devotion to the world's wild cats and his unsurpassed conservation efforts.

Nemmers, Sherry, "Wanted: Missing Cat." Sherry, Executive Creative Director, EVP, for New York City based global ad agencies and private consultant, has created this one-page bulletin on the missing puma in the east that can be copied for distribution.

Noss, Reed, "Fire in Florida and the Southeastern Coastal Plain." Noss, is a writer, photographer, lecturer, and consultant in natural history, ecology, and conservation and serves as Chief Science Advisor for the Southeastern Grasslands Initiative and the Endangered Ecosystems Alliance.

Parsons, Dave, "The Saga of the Mexican Gray Wolf (el lobo)." Parsons, the Carnivore Conservation Biologist with TRI and Project Coyote, tells the story of Mexican wolves in the United States and of their remarkable reintroduction twenty years ago.

Proescholdt, Kevin, "Wilderness Giant Stewart "Brandy" Brandborg Moves on at 93." Proescholdt, Conservation Director of Wilderness Watch, presents a loving tribute to Brandy.

Project Coyote, "Join 65 Scientists in Opposing the U.S. Predator Challenge." An action alert from Project Coyote and

Dave Parsons to request signatures to express opposition to a proposed nationwide coyote killing contest.

Project Coyote, film, "Killing Games, Wildlife in the Crosshairs." Showing in Albuquerque and in Massachusetts.

Rewilding Earth Editors, "Arctic National Wildlife Refuge Letter of Support." Editors write this letter register our strong opposition to any oil and gas exploration or exploration in America's landmark reserve, the Arctic Refuge, background appears in Brad Meiklejohn's article, "It's Your Refuge."

Rewilding Earth Editors, "Project Coyote, Promoting Coexistence Between People & Wildlife." Highlighting Project Coyote's good work to protect coyotes and other wildlife.

Rewilding Earth Editors, "Roadless Rule Letter Opposing State of Alaska's Petition for Exemption."

Robinson, Kirk, "It's Time for a Revolution in State Wildlife Governance." The Founder and Executive Director of Western Wildlife Conservancy writes that the bottom line is that state wildlife management agencies and the special interests they serve function as a cartel to protect their grip on wildlife management at the expense of the integrity, stability and beauty of biotic communities and in violation of the public trust.

Robinson, Kirk and Dave Parsons, "Wildlife Governance Reform: Where to Begin." Robinson and Dave Parsons report on the conference held in Albuquerque in mid-August, "Wildlife for All: Re-envisioning State Wildlife Governance" and call for wildlife governance reform on the national and state level.

Rosemarino, Nicole, "Bringing Back the American Serengeti." The Executive Director of Southern Plains Land Trust, presents the profile of SPLT, their history, goals, and work to protect the shortgrass prairies of the southern Great Plains.

Sakashita, Miyoko, "How We Fight Trump's Dirty Drilling Plan for our Oceans." The Oceans Director and Senior Counsel for Center for Biological Diversity, says the Trump drive for energy dominance seeks to transform every wild oceanscape into an industrial wasteland.

Sayen, Jamie, "Who Speaks for Nash Stream Forest." Sayen, Northeast writer and conservation activist, describes the unresolved attempt to protect 67,000 acres of New Hampshire managed forest.

Silbert, Shelley and Lauren Berutich, "Strategic Defense in Wildly Challenging Times." The Executive Director and Grassroots Leadership Director for Great Old Broads for Wilderness, propose specific steps to focus our energies on the many challenges to conservation and protection of public lands.

Solomon, Christopher, "The World's Wilderness: Going, Going, and Soon Gone." Repost from *Outside Magazine*, Solomon writes that the world's last, big wildlands are disappearing at an alarming rate and proposes options to reverse this trend.

Soulé, Michael, "A National Corridors Campaign for Restoring America the Beautiful." Soulé writes that many conservation biologists would define success as the protection of inter-connected lands and waters that provide sufficient habitat and security for vigorous and well-distributed populations of all native species and the restoration of ecological functions provided by them.

Soulé, Michael, "Surrendering." A poem by our dear friend and father of conservation biology.

Smith, Danna, "To Solve the Climate Crisis We Must Stand for Forests and Re-Wild America." Smith, Director, Dogwood Alliance, calls for forest protection to become a national climate priority.

Spahr, Terry, "Daring to Tell the Truth about Sustainability." The producer of *8 Billion Angels,* argues that we are outstripping our planet's resources and emitting waste faster than the earth can regenerate those resources or absorb those wastes.

Spatz, Chris and John Laundré, "The Ecological Imperative for a National Cougar Recovery Plan, Part 1 & 2," Spatz, executive director of the Cougar Rewilding Foundation, and John

Laundré', vice president of the Cougar Rewilding Foundation who has studied cougars for over twenty years, describe challenges and potential for bringing cougars back to the Northeast.

Swift, Ken, "CATRUNNERS, Prologue." Swift presents a make-believe adventure for youth of all ages, human and feline.

Vacariu, Kim, "To Win, Conservationists Must Change Their Message." Vacariu, former Western Director of Wildlands Network and communication specialist, argues that conservationists must deliver new messages that subtly justify pro-Nature voting actions to the non-conservation voting public. Also included is "Branding for Biodiversity," an interview with Sherry Nemmers, about how to communicate in favor of conservation.

Wilderness Watch, "Don't Let Notorious Anti-Wilderness Utah Politicians Wreck the San Rafael Swell and Desolation Canyon!" Action alert.

Wilderness Watch, "Help Protect our Largest Wilderness Study Area." Action alert to protect Chugach National Forest roadless area.

Wilderness Watch, "Keep up the Pressure to Prevent Cruelty in our National Preserves." Action alert to alert readers to summit comments to the NPS again the proposed roll-back of the NPS rule that banned controversial hunting practices on 19 million acres of America's National Preserves in Alaska, which includes millions of acres of Wilderness.

Wildlands Network, "Wildlife Corridors Conservation Act of 2018." Action alert requesting help to spread the word about this recently introduced legislation.

Wuerthner, George, "BLM Under Trump and Zinke: A Disaster for Public Lands." Ecologist, writer, and speaker for Wilderness Watch in the "Wilderness Under Siege," writes that the Trump administration is "characterized as reducing all regulations, enhancing opportunities for private profit and development at public expense, and giving away as much of the public domain and resources as possible."

Wuerthner, George, and Brian Miller, "Climate Change and Freshwater Realities." Wuerthner and Miller discuss how population and agriculture drive climate change.

Wuerthner, George, "House Version of the Farm Bill Contains Anti-Environmental Provisions – Call your Senator today!" This is an action alert for calls to our Senators as the Farm Bill moves into conference committee. The House Version contains a provision to speed logging in the West under the guise of reducing large wildfires, and it reduces the requirement for NEPA and expands the use of "Categorical Exclusions."

Animal Welfare Institute, "US Fish & Wildlife Service Plan Dooms Remaining Wild Red Wolves to Extinction." Action Center alert from Animal Welfare Institute.

Wuerthner, George, "Wilderness Under Siege." A talk by George given around the country alerting readers to the current threats that wilderness was facing last year.

York, Suzanne, "Why Family Planning is Good for People and the Planet." The Director of Transition Earth argues that we must find the political and Societal/cultural will to attain a healthy population number.

ABOUT THE REWILDING BOOKSTORE

The Rewilding Bookstore features titles by leaders of The Rewilding Institute, important books by friends of the Institute willing to list their titles, and recommended reading by Institute staff and board. The bookstore also offers reviews of important books relevant to rewilding and related topics. We are expanding our booklist to include new and old titles to inspire and inform readers, and we welcome any suggestions you may have.

Readers may order through the Rewilding Earth website (rewilding.org) by going to "Bookstore" in the menu. If you have any questions about ordering featured titles, please contact Roxanne Pacheco at TRI@rewilding.org or call at 505-288-9231. Thank you very much for supporting our authors and The Rewilding Institute.

Books For Sale

Rewilding North America: A Vision for Conservation in the 21st Century, by Dave Foreman.
Unmatched for its deep, thorough look at extinction and how humans make it happen; and what conservation biology teaches us about wild things and how to keep them wild. Foreman offers a mind-opening vision for rewilding North America grounded in a North American Wildlands Network. Though *Rewilding* is not an academic book, it is being used as a text in many colleges and universities. Island Press, 2004. 295 pages, index, footnotes, maps, tables. Paperback $35, Hardcover $60.

Man Swarm and the Killing of Wildlife, by Dave Foreman with Laura Carroll.

The first edition of *Man Swarm* reached the conservationist community; in this new and updated edition, Dave Foreman and seasoned editor Laura Carroll expand the readership to the masses. This tight second edition: lays out how the overpopulation explosion is still with us, smartly challenges those who don't believe overpopulation is real, shows that overpopulation is solvable, takes an ecological stand on immigration and its reform in the U.S. as part of the solution, and gives tangible ways all people can be part of the solution. 2014, 196 pages, Paperback $20.

Man Swarm and the Killing of Wildlife, by Dave Foreman.

Human overpopulation—man swarm—is the main driver behind the biodiversity crisis—the greatest mass extinction since the dinosaurs' demise, the scalping of hundreds of millions of acres of forest and other key wildlife habitat, and the atmospheric pollution by greenhouse gases leading to "Global Weirding." Only by stabilizing human population worldwide and in the United States can we stop wrecking our home—Earth. Foreman outlines a sweep of practical steps we can take to bring our numbers down to what Earth can support—if we have the daring, boldness, and love of life to do it. First in the For the Wild Things series. Raven's Eye Press, 2011. 274 pages, index, appendices, graphs, tables. Paperback $20.

The Lobo Outback Funeral Home: A Novel, by Dave Foreman.

Foreword by Doug Peacock (paperback only). *Lobo* is the only novel that tells the story of conservation from inside the conservation family. Set in southwestern New Mexico, it's the tale of a tough, winsome conservation biologist, the wolves she loves and studies, the man who loves both her and the wolves but who can't find the strength to make a commitment, and the wolf-hating local lowlifes and their rich rancher leader. Sex, violence, wolves, wilderness. 226 pages. Johnson Books, 2004, University Press of Colorado, 2000, First Edition Hardcover $20.

Take Back Conservation, by Dave Foreman.

Aldo Leopold wrote, "There are some who can live without wild things, and some who cannot." *Take Back Conservation* is for those who cannot live without wild things, who are the heart and soul of the wilderness and wildlife conservation movement. Second in the For the Wild Things series. Raven's Eye Press, 2012, 375 pages, index, glossary. Paperback $25.

Confessions of an Eco-Warrior, by Dave Foreman.

Part memoir, part history of Earth First!, and a rousing heartfelt call to save wild things, *Confessions of an Eco-Warrior* is a landmark of conservation writing. "One of the towering figures, the mighty sequoias, of American conservation...."— Bill McKibben. Out of print, few copies left, First Edition (1991) Hardcover for collectors. Harmony, 1991, 229 pages, index. $75.

The Big Outside: A Descriptive Inventory of the Big Wilderness Areas of the U. S. First Edition by Dave Foreman and Howie Wolke. Foreword by Michael Frome.

A legendary, broad study of the big roadless areas in the United States: 100,000 acres and over in the West, 50,000 acres and over in the East (368 areas in all described). Includes Bob Marshall's 1927 and 1936 roadless area inventories. Both the first and second editions of *The Big Outside* have long been out of print. 458 pages, photos, maps, research sources. Ned Ludd Books, 1988, First Edition, Paperback, $50.

Split Rock Wildway: Scouting the Adirondack Park's Most Diverse Wildlife Corridor, by John Davis.

A rambling look at some of the charismatic and enigmatic wildlife thriving in the wooded hills and adjacent waterways linking Lake Champlain with the High Peaks. Author John Davis and artist friends illustrate the ecological importance, conservation value, and natural beauty of the wildway and its many creatures. Residents and visitors alike will grow a little closer to their permanent or occasional wild neighbors, from salamanders to sturgeon to raptors to moose, as they stroll through the pages of Split Rock Wildway. This book is intended to help better protect the lands and waters of Split Rock Wildway and the larger Adirondack Park. It is generously sponsored by Eddy Foundation, with a portion of sales benefiting Champlain Area Trails, Northeast Wilderness Trust, and other conservation groups. Essex Editions, 2017, 157 pages, Paperback, $15

Big, Wild, and Connected, by John Davis.

In 2011, adventurer and conservationist John Davis walked, cycled, skied, canoed, and kayaked on an epic 10-month, 7,600-mile journey that took him from the Florida Keys to a remote seashore on the Gaspe Peninsula of Quebec. Davis was motivated by a dream: to see a continent-long corridor conserved for wildlife in the eastern United States and Canada, especially for the large carnivores so critical to the health of the land. In *Big, Wild, and Connected*, we travel the Eastern Wildway with Davis, viscerally experiencing the challenges large carnivores, with their need for vast territories, face in an ongoing search for food, water, shelter, and mates. On his self-propelled journey, Davis explores the wetlands, forests, and peaks that are the last strongholds for wildlife in the East. This includes strategically important segments of disturbed landscapes, from longleaf pine savanna in the Florida Panhandle to road-latticed woods of Pennsylvania. Despite the challenges, Davis argues that creation of an Eastern Wildway is within our reach and would serve as a powerful symbol of our natural and cultural heritage. *Big, Wild, and Connected* reveals Eastern landscapes through wild eyes, a reminder that, for the creatures with which we share the land, movement is as essential to life as air, water, and food. Davis' journey shows that a big, wild, and connected network of untamed places is the surest way to ensure wildlife survival through the coming centuries. Island Press, 2015, 212 pages, Paperback $15

Moral Ground: Ethical Action for a Planet in Peril, edited by Kathleen Dean Moore and Michael P. Nelson. Foreword by Desmond Tutu.

Sweeping in depth, breadth, thought, and feeling, eighty women and men answer whether we have a "moral obligation to protect the future of a planet in peril." Dave Foreman's short essay, "Wild Things for Their Own Sakes," builds on Darwin and Leopold to be a bedrock stand for the inborn good of wild things. Others answer from intrinsic, humanistic, and practical overlooks. Among them are Barack Obama, John Paul II, Dalai Lama, Ursula Le Guin, Barbara Kingsolver, Terry Tempest Williams, E. O. Wilson, Gary Snyder, and others from all over Earth. Trinity University Press, 2010, 478 pages, authors' bios. Hardcover $25.

The Way of Natural History, edited by Thomas Lowe Fleischner.

Once, biology was natural history, done mostly in the field. Now biology is done indoor mostly by "lab rats." In some universities, one can get a biology degree without doing anything outside. This fading of natural history is a harsh threat to our tie to wild things in wildlands and –seas and to our work to keep and bring back the whole Tree of Life. Fleischner, retired from Prescott College, and fellow biologists and conservationists call for coming home to the mindfulness of natural history. Dave Foreman's little essay, "Talking to Wild Things," builds on Leopold and asks us to get out and meet our wild neighbors in wild neighborhoods as a fellow neighbor or a wayfarer. Among the other twenty-one writers are Robert Aitken, Alison Deming, Kathleen Dean Moore, Bob Pyle, and Steve Trombulak. Trinity University Press, 2011, 218 pages, authors' bios, Paperback, $17.

Continental Conservation: Scientific Foundations of Regional Reserve Networks, edited by Michael Soulé and John Terborgh.

Scientifically solid and highly readable, *Continental Conservation* is an anthology written by the top conservation biologists in the U.S., Canada, and Mexico explaining why conservation must be done on a continental scale. It covers the need for big predators; the need for big wilderness areas and how to best design them; the importance of wildlife movement linkages, ecological and evolutionary processes of wildlife, flooding, and predation; and much more. Soulé and Terborgh give a warm-hearted, tough-minded call to save wild things and their wilderness homes. Island Press/Wildlands Project, 1999, 227 pages, index, footnotes, some illustrations. Paperback, $20.

ABOUT ESSEX EDITIONS

Essex Editions is an independent press located on the Adirondack shores of Lake Champlain.

We are creators.
> *Mavericks.*
> *Risk-takers.*
> *Adventurers.*
> *Connectors.*
> *Collectors.*
> *Curators.*
> *Catalysts.*
> *Incubators.*
We are storytellers.

Part artisanal publisher and part transmedia consultancy, Essex Editions collaborates with authors, artists, and activists who believe that storytelling should be innovative, provocative, culturally enriching, and ecologically responsible.

Learn more at essexeditions.com.

SPONSORS

The generous support of Rewilding Earth's donor foundations, corporations, and individuals underpins our recent success in launching a vibrant online pub (rewilding.org), and now in showcasing some of our most notable contributions in this anthology. We would like to thank this wild bunch of conservation leaders and to briefly single out for praise several sponsors helping to make possible this first edition of Rewilding Earth Unplugged. We encourage you to support these truly green businesses. Please contact us about becoming a Rewilding Earth sponsor via our website or you can send mail to The Rewilding Institute, P.O. Box 13768, Albuquerque, NM 87192.

BIOHABITATS

Biohabitats

In the early 1980s, an outdoorsy, nature-loving undergrad named Keith Bowers had an epiphany. Keith had been studying landscape architecture at the University of Virginia when he met Ed Garbisch, a pioneering practitioner of marsh restoration along the Chesapeake Bay. "Wait a minute," thought Keith. "I can apply my education to restoring the places I love?" After graduating in 1982, Keith started Biohabitats, an ecological restoration company. 36 years later, with a mission to "restore the earth and inspire ecological stewardship," Biohabitats has become one of the most recognized names in ecological restoration and conservation.

Biohabitats applies the science of ecology to restore ecosystems, conserve habitat, and regenerate the natural systems that sustain all life on Earth. They do this through assessment, research, planning, design, engineering, and construction. Since the firm's early days improving the ecosystems and watersheds of the Chesapeake, Biohabitats now operates out of seven bioregion offices in the U.S., helping communities all over the world to protect wildlife habitat, conserve water, enhance biodiversity, plan for the future in ways that enhance ecology and resilience, and link the natural world and its systems with the built environment. Behind this work is an intention to respect Earth's ecological limit, heal ecological processes, and catalyze mutually beneficial relationships among the land and all forms of life.

Diverse in background and discipline, Biohabitats team

members are unified by a shared set of values. "Revere Wild Nature" is one of them. The firm not only works to protect wild nature in all types of environments, but turns to it as a guide for conserving, restoring, and regenerating the full expression of biological diversity and ecosystem functions to ensure our survival.

A purpose-driven company that believes in the power of business to catalyze good, Biohabitats measures success primarily by the degree to which their work enhances biodiversity, ecological democracy, and the resilience of life. A certified B Corporation®, member of 1% for the Planet, and recipient of the JUST™ label.

Learn more at biohabitats.com and find them @Biohabitats on Facebook, Twitter, LinkedIn, and Instagram.

FOUNDATION EARTH

foundation
EARTH

Rethinking society from the ground up!

Foundation Earth is a national, non-profit, public interest advocacy organization founded in 2011. Our focus includes: economic models, technology, biospheric education, and earth jurisprudence. We call for a rethink of society from the ground up. We envision more self-reliant communities embedded in a continental network of bioregional economies. Time is not on our side. A rapid shift from an industrial society that ignores nature's carrying capacity limits and irresponsibly pollutes (cheater economics) to a True Cost Economy will require examining the dimensions of a deeply resilient economy, arguing for it, and providing advisory services to social movements concerning systems change. Our mission is to bring an earth-centered "True Cost Economy" into reality.

Learn more at fdnearth.org and find them @FoundationEarth on Facebook and Twitter.

KAHTOOLA

Kahtoola makes outdoor gear that allows people to explore and enjoy wild and beautiful places. Based in Flagstaff, AZ, and surrounded by the sublime geology, wildlife, and open spaces of the Colorado Plateau, we are afforded endless opportunities for adventure. Inspiration can be discovered around every canyon bend, along each stretch of river, among its stunning rock formations, and by immersing oneself in its vast landscapes. It is this inspiration that drives our passion to advocate for protecting and preserving public lands not only for future generations of people, but the wildlife that lives on them.

Currently, Kahtoola is banding together with others in support of ongoing Native American efforts to make permanent the standing 20-year ban on uranium mining around the Grand Canyon. If not stopped, contamination from existing and new mining claims would have irreversible, adverse effects on the area's watershed, diversity of wildlife, a community of indigenous people, and the place we call home.

Learn more at kahtoola.com and find them @Kahtoola on Facebook, Twitter, LinkedIn, and Instagram.

PATAGONIA

patagonia®

Patagonia is an outdoor apparel company based in Ventura, California. Since 1973, activism has been at the heart of the company's work by supporting efforts to defend our air, land and water around the globe. Through a self-imposed Earth tax, 1% for the Planet, Patagonia has funded thousands of environmental nonprofits and can count contributions of more than $100 million in grants and in-kind donations to date to local organizations.

Learn more at patagonia.com and find them @Patagonia on Facebook, Twitter, LinkedIn, and Instagram.

Made in the USA
Columbia, SC
10 June 2019